Pretending at Home

SUNY Series, Children's Play in Society
Anthony D. Pellegrini, editor

PRETENDING AT HOME
Early Development in a Sociocultural Context

Wendy L. Haight and Peggy J. Miller

State University of New York Press

A modified and condensed version of Chapters 4-6 appeared as
"The Development of everyday pretend play:
A Longitudinal Study of Mothers' participation in *Merrill-Palmer Quarterly*, 38 (2), 331-349

Permission to reprint figure 4.2 granted by
Merrill-Palmer Quarterly

Published by
State University of New York Press, Albany

For information, address the State University of New York Press,
State University Plaza, Albany, NY 12246

Production by Christine Lynch
Marketing by Bernadette LaManna

Library of Congress Cataloging-in-Publication Data

Haight, Wendy L., 1958—
    Pretending at home: Early development in sociocultural context
  Wendy L. Haight and Peggy J. Miller.
      p. cm. — (SUNY series, children's play in society)
    Includes bibliographical references and index.
    ISBN 0-7914-1471-X (cloth). — ISBN 0-7914-1472-8 (pbk.)
    1. Play 2. Symbolic play. I. Miller, Peggy J. (Peggy Jo),
  1950— . II. Title. III. Series.
  HQ782.H335 1993
  155.4'18—dc20   92-22784
                                                                  CIP

10 9 8 7 6 5 4 3 2 1

We dedicate this book to our children

Matthew and Camilla
&
Kurt and Kathleen

Acknowledgments

Financial support for this project has come primarily from the Spencer Foundation, in the form of a dissertation year fellowship to Wendy Haight. This manuscript has benefited greatly from the constructive comments on earlier drafts by Catherine Garvey, Ross Parke, and Barbara Rogoff. Brenda Barton-Taylor helped tremendously with reliability checking, coding, and transcribing. The cover photo as well as the other professional photos appearing in the book were taken by Bridget Nagel. Finally, this project would not have been possible without the families who generously allowed us into their homes.

Contents

1

Introduction

Three-year-old Nancy and her mother are in the basement playroom fixing decorations for a Halloween party. When Nancy begins to show signs of boredom, her mother suggests that she drive her car. Nancy retrieves a childsized red plastic dashboard with steering wheel and seatbelt, and positions herself for driving. "Be sure to fasten your seat belt, right?" reminds her mother, "Buckle up for safety!" Nancy fastens her seat belt, turns the steering wheel, and pushes the horn. To her mother's queries, "Where are you going? Are you taking a trip?" Nancy replies, "To Havana." Again?" asks her mother, "Where did you learn about Havana?" Nancy continues to steer the car while demonstrating how to drive, "You drive a car like this. Like this. OK?" She explains that Havana is far away and discusses with her mother how many stops will be needed en route, and how old one has to be to get a driver's license.

Eventually Nancy's mother ceases to be a spectator to her daughter's play and actually enters the pretend world in the role of passenger. Nancy tells her to sit in the back seat and buckle her seat belt. Her mother then asks, "Are you the mom?" and Nancy says, "Yes." This exchange establishes Nancy's mother in the pretend role of child, while Nancy herself assumes the role of mother. That is, the role relationship that ordinarily applies has been reversed in play: mother has become child and child has become mother. The pretend child proceeds to badger the placidly driving pretend mother: she wants to open the car window and stick her feet out, complains that a bug flew in the window, whines about being hungry, and finally announces an urgent need to go to the bathroom. The pretend mother utters an exasperated, "Ohhhh!," stops the car, and shows the child to the bathroom (the area to the left of the sofa). Toileting accomplished, complete with sound effects and enacted flushing, the pair get back into the car and resume their journey. The pretend child is now tired and wants to go to sleep but continues to chatter, and the pretend mother, vigorously steering, scolds her in a stern voice, "And don't make any noise!" This admonition proves ineffective. The pretend child thinks she might tickle her mother, complains of being bored, and demands a snack. At last, nearly ten minutes after departing, the harassed mother and the fidgeting child arrive at their destination. The pretend mother declares, "We're here! . . . OK! And the results . . . And here (pointing to a pillow on the sofa) are the statues!" The two then proceed to explore Havana. When the pretend child attempts to step back into the real world in order to finish the laundry, the distraught mother locks her in an imaginary bathroom. A series of pretend negotiations follow and, eventually washing the real clothes is incorporated into the pretend scenerio as the two tourists explore how the Cubans do their laundry.

* * *

This book traces the development of pretend play in nine children growing up within educated, middle-class European American families. As the opening scene illustrates, the development of pretend play is embedded within a distinctive sociocultural context. First, pretend play emerges within particular physical ecologies. Nancy is pretending in a room set aside for play, surrounded by objects—play dashboards, baby dolls, miniature cars—suggestive of pretend themes. Second, pretend play emerges within particular social ecologies. Nancy pretends primarily with other people and, through the age of three, her mother is her main play partner. Third, pretend play is governed by social and communicative conventions. Nancy and her mother conduct their play according to norms of mutuality, agreeing upon role assignments, informing one another about shifts in scene, and negotiating departures from the pretend frame. Finally, pretend play is informed by a broader system of beliefs. In casual conversations with the first author, Nancy's mother expressed the opinion that pretending is important to children's development, and that parents can facilitate their children's pretending.

The sociocultural perspective of pretending presented in this book addresses issues central to understanding both development and culture. We view pretend play as an early manfestation of the basic human capacity for mythmaking, upon which culture depends. "To be human and to live in a meaningful way within a culture requires living in and through a very sophisticated, abstract system that is largely imaginary" (Vandenberg, 1986, p. 7). In playing with particular myths—of family or Superheroes, for example—children not only become more deeply rooted in a system of meanings but alter, comment upon, and reinterpret meaning.

> This tension between the myths imposed from without and the exertion of personal control in shaping one's interpretation and use of the

myths reflects the poles of a dialectic relationship between the individual and his culture. Through play, the child is socialized into a general cultural framework while developing a unique individuality with a distinctly personal matrix of life history and lived meanings. (p. 8)

This dialectic between individual and culture is articulated in more general terms by anthropologists Bauman and Sherzer (1989). They claim that "the dynamic interplay between the social, conventional, ready-made in social life and the individual, creative and emergent qualities of human existence" (p. xix) is a crucial problem in the social disciplines. These kindred perspectives suggest that our understanding of children and of culture ultimately will be enriched by the study of pretend play.

An integrated understanding of developmental and cultural dimensions of pretend play, however, has been slow in coming. As Schwartzman (1980) has pointed out, studies of play and studies of culture have tended to develop as separate enterprises, reflecting the intellectual histories of psychology and anthropology as distinct disciplines. Developmental psychologists have been interested in pretend play primarily as an index, and possible facilitator of, cognitive development, emotional well-being, creativity, and problem solving. Anthropologists have been interested in pretend play as a means by which children are socialized into culture. In this book we hope to contribute to a more integrated understanding of pretend play as both a developmental and a cultural phenomenon.

A second factor that has obscured the cultural nature of pretend play has been the overwhelming predominance of mainstream American children as the subject population in psychological studies of pretending. When researcher, reader, and subjects of a study share an implicit cultural framework, a "paradox of familiarity" operates against articulation of that framework (Ochs and Schieffelin 1984). Fortunately, there is a growing body of cross-cultural research that makes it possible to compare middle-class European American children with their counterparts in other cultural communities. By adopting a comparative perspective on the very group that has been studied most we hope to gain insight into the cultural nature of pretending.

A keystone of our empirical approach has been to describe the sociocultural context within which pretending occurs. Most of what is known about the emergence and early development of pretend play derives from studies that have examined pretending under quasi-experimental conditions in laboratory playrooms. Surprisingly little is known about pretending in everyday life—even for mainstream American children. We attempt to redress this imbalance by observing children as they go about their ordinary activities in and around the home. Our nine subjects are the offspring of well-educated, European American parents who live in spacious apartments or houses in affluent urban neighborhoods. Because each child was observed repeatedly from one to four years of age, we have gained an understanding not only of group patterns but of the individuality that gets expressed in pretend play. Although most of our young pretenders did some travelling, Nancy was the only one with a passion for Havana.

Our descriptions of these children are framed in terms of several important issues and theoretical questions. One basic issue concerns the amount of time that young children spend pretending. Claims that pretend play has a salutary effect on development rest on the implicit assumption that pretending is a major occupation of young children. Is this assumption warranted? We found that the children did, in fact, spend a significant amount of their daily time pretending.

A related issue concerns the nature of pretend episodes. When children are observed continuously for three to four hours at a stretch, it is possible to preserve the integrity of pretend episodes—how they get started, how they unfold, how they terminate, how long they last. Also preserved are the circumstances that occasion episodes of pretending, raising questions about the expressive, didactic, and recreational funtions of everyday pretending. To our knowledge this is the first attempt to document how pretend activity emerges from the ongoing domestic scene.

Although we consider these issues to be fundamental, the primary objective of this book is to address questions that converge on the sociocultural nature of pretending. Leading theories of pretend play are most powerful in their formulations of the cognitive and affective dimensions of pretending (Piaget 1962; Winnicott 1971) and least well developed with respect to the social and cultural. There is, however, an emerging literature relevant to these neglected dimensions, and detectable within it are several levels of sociocultural analysis. These levels of analysis have to do with the physical and social ecologies in which pretend play is embedded, the belief systems that frame and inform the practice of pretend play, and the cultural conventions by which pretending is conducted.

The Physical Ecology

One important way in which culture affects pretend play is through the arrangement of the physical context. The families we describe contrast sharply with families from other cultural groups where manufactured toys are scarce, for example, rural Indian and rural Guatamalan groups (Goncu, Rogoff, and Mistry, 1989). The domestic environments we observed were arranged so as to accommodate the storage and use of large quantities of toys and other play props—dolls and doll houses; action figures and pirate sets; pony castles; Lego building sets with people, miniature trains, airplanes, and automobiles; stuffed animals; tents and playhouses; and bride, Superman, Ninja turtle, and kitty cat costumes. By providing their children with an abundance of objects specialized for use in play, caregivers both communicate that pretend play is a valued activity, and exert a powerful indirect influence on its development (Sutton-Smith 1986).

The Social Ecology

Another important way in which culture affects pretend play is through the assignment of categories of persons to settings and activites (Whiting and Edwards 1988; Goodnow 1990). Whether other persons are available as potential play partners and what sorts of persons—mothers, fathers, siblings—are available, depend on routine arrangements of time and space, with their concomitant distributions of persons. By observing young children in the family context we discovered that pretending was not only overwhelmingly social but that mothers served as the primary play partners from one to three years of age. Given the economic activites and childcare arrangements in these families, children had much greater opportunity to pretend with mothers than with fathers, siblings, or friends.

The Conduct of Social Pretend Play

Pretend play is cultural not only at the levels of physical and social ecology. It is also a conventionalized expressive system. This is perhaps most apparent with respect to content. Children enact the familiar roles and daily routines that reflect community norms and values. Vygotsky (1978) described pretend play as based on implicit rules of social behavior. By pretending, children come to better understand these cultural norms. In the opening example of role play between Nancy and her mother, Vygotsky would see an opportunity for Nancy to become aware of the rules and responsibilities of motherly behavior that she is not consciously aware of in real situations. As she pretends to be a mother and attempts to pacify a cranky and demanding child, she gains new insight into the mother-child relationship.

The creation of a pretend world requires a specialized set of communicative conventions for marking a nonliteral orientation and for negotiating and assigning roles, transforming objects and locations, and enacting scenarios (Bateson 1956; El'Konin 1966; Garvey 1982, 1990; Schwartzman 1978). Garvey and Kramer (1989) recently argued that the language of pretend play is not simply an outcome of ordinary language development but represents a specialized use of language that develops over the preschool period. The conventionalized form of these communications strongly suggests that they are learned through interaction with more experienced players.

This insight, along with our finding that mothers pretended extensively with their young children, led us to ask a number of specific questions about mothers' participation and how it affected the formation of pretend episodes. These analyses revealed that mothers systematically introduced the pretend mode and established, in interaction with the child, conventions for the social conduct of pretense. Mothers did not impose the pretend mode on disinterested children; instead, like Nancy and her mother, they constructed norms of mutual engagement. Both mothers and children initiated episodes and together they expressed and manipulated topics of mutual concern—sibling rivalry, the child's fears, parent-child power relations, and rules and rule transgressions. Mothers attended to and pursued the topics introduced by the child, while at the same time extending the play by elaborating upon and prompting the child. Moreover, we found that the caregivers' participation had effects on the episode itself. Episodes with mothers were more sustained than solo episodes, and children incorporated what their mothers had said earlier in the episode into their own subsequent responses.

Belief Systems

The contexts and conduct of pretending are framed and informed by a system of beliefs about adult-child relationships in general, and play in particular. In some cultures, such as the Yucatec Mayan (Gaskins 1990), parental beliefs about childrearing and the nature of children preclude parental participation in children's play. By contrast, educated European American mothers and fathers typically believe that pretend play is important to children's development and that their participation is appropriate and facilitative (Haight 1991). Although the current study did not include an inquiry into parental beliefs and values, chapter 10 summarizes results from Haight's (1991) study of the beliefs of a similar sample of parents.

Although the main patterns emerged quite strongly, we were also struck by the extent of individual variation within this homogeneous sample of middle-class families. Children differed among themselves, and mothers differed among themselves, not just quantitatively but qualitatively. It was obvious, as we looked on, that some mothers and children not only pretended more prolifically than others but with more originality and inventiveness. It was obvious that some mothers and children found pretend play less appealing than book reading or coloring, whereas for others it was a favored and highly satisfying mode of relating. Existing theories cannot account for this kind of individual variation. Nor can they account for cultural variation. Although our study is not comparative in design, it is informed by a cross-cultural literature. Clearly, the case that we describe is extreme in the extent to which early pretending is encouraged. Not only is maternal time, attention, and imagination devoted to pretending, but large sets of toys specialized for pretending are lavished on young children.

In summary, the purpose of this book is to describe the emergence and early development of pretend play in its sociocultural context. In the next chapter we begin by describing the children and their families, and elaborate upon the advantages of using a naturalistic approach to address the questions at hand. The issue of how frequently children pretend is taken up in chapter 3 and procedures for defining and quantifying episodes of pretend play are set forth. The findings reported in chapter 3 are important not only in their own right but because the episodes that are extracted provide the basis for the analyses reported in succeeding chapters. Chapters 4, 5, and 6 establish the social nature of pretend play by describing its interpersonal context, the social conduct of mother- child pretending, and the effects of the partner's participation on pretend episodes. Chapter 7 complements these chapters by examining the social functions of pretending, providing qualitative descriptions of the interpersonal circumstances out of which pretending arises. Chapter 8 describes play objects and other aspects of the physical ecology of pretend play, revealing still other social and cultural dimensions of pretend play. In an effort to provide a more integrated view of our findings and to illustrate individual variation in pretending, we present in chapter 9 portraits of pretending in two of the children. Conclusions and directions for future research are presented in chapter 10.

2

Studying Everyday Pretending

It is late morning. Three-year-old Molly and her five-year-old sister Rachael are lying side by side on their bedroom floor (ostensibly "picking up"). Molly asks repeatedly to play with Rachael's Tropical Skipper doll, but Rachael refuses. Eventually, the distraught Molly bites Rachael, who authoritatively reminds her of the prohibition on biting and then threatens to "tell." Molly explains, "I'm a doggie who bites." Rachael begins to scold the doggie and then realizes, "Baby doggies don't like Tropical Skipper!" Apparently satisfied that the issue is resolved, she turns away and begins to sing, "The sound of music!"

Molly, however, is still angry and scratches her on the back. Rachael grabs the front of Molly's dress, "You are a cheese cracker that I bite." Molly laughs. Rachael: "You are a cheese cracker that I bite if you bite me again!" Molly laughs again. Rachael refers to Molly as "doggie" and scrapes her with the toy comb. Molly complains, "I don't want to do it else I'll bite you again!" Rachael: "And then you'll be my cheese cracker who I bite. And I really will bite you!" Molly and Rachael move very close together, faces almost touching, and make biting gestures and noises. Rachael: "I'm gonna bite you if you bite me again. And you will be a cheese cracker that I will really bite."

Then, smiling and gazing at Rachael, Molly bites Tropical Skipper's feet, gently. Rachael grabs Tropical Skipper from Molly, "Noo!" Rachael smiles, then continues in a sing-song, authoritative tone, "Don't ever bite on Barbie's feet. How would you like it if somebody came up and bited on your feet? Tropical Skipper doesn't like it. How would you like it if she came up and ate, bited on your foot. And now here she comes to." Rachael holds Molly's leg up at the ankle. Molly points her toe towards Tropical Skipper's mouth. Rachael makes eating noises as she holds Tropical Skipper to Molly's toe. Molly: "She didn't eat up my foot." Rachael: "Well she bited it. Well she did bite it." Molly laughs then picks up her blanket and walks away.

* * *

This episode illustrates the emotional intensity that often characterizes everyday pretending. It also illustrates how pretending evolves out of ongoing activities: in this case pretending was occasioned by sibling conflict over the prized Tropical Skipper doll, conflict that gets carried over into the pretense. A precarious balance is maintained between really biting and pretending to bite, between hostile and amused feelings. Admission into this intimate, imaginary world requires time and discretion. The observer recorded this episode on videotape while she was positioned across the bedroom in the doorway of an open closet. She had been recording for two consecutive hours and had spent approximately twenty hours videotaping in the home prior to this observation session. The children were comfortable enough in her presence to engage in activities that are generally disapproved of by adults (e.g., arguing and biting), and they seemed to respect her role as observer, approaching her only occasionally for help with dressing a doll. In this chapter we briefly describe the children and their families, and the methods that were used to obtain a record of everyday pretending.

The Children and Their Families

We recruited nine children and their mothers through newspaper ads. The four girls and five boys were similar in many respects to other children typically studied in research on pretend play: they were from families who had the time and space for pretending and the financial resources to provide an abundance of toys and play props. Six of the families lived in an academic community in Chicago, and three lived in a nearby suburb. All of the parents were college educated and ranged in age from their early twenties to their early forties. The fathers were social workers, lawyers, a physician, a graduate student, a businessman, and a college professor. With one exception, the mothers had pursued professions before their children were born. They were social workers, teachers, a businesswoman, a photojournalist, and a computer programmer. At the time of the study, the mothers were the primary caregivers. Three children had older siblings, three had younger siblings, two had a younger and an older sibling, and one was an only child.

The Research Strategy

The study was longitudinal in design and naturalistic in approach, involving a succession of extended observations of the children in the contexts of everyday family life. Our methods combined several features designed to maximize the ecological and cultural validity of the findings.

   Naturalistic observational approach. Previous developmental studies of pretend play typically have examined play under quasi-experimental conditions in laboratory playrooms. By contrast, in the present study we observed pretending under the conditions in which it ordinarily occurs—at home, on the playground, on the way to the grocery store—with family members and friends near at hand. A naturalistic approach was best suited to our goal of documenting the social ecology and routine conduct of everyday pretending. Also, our approach is compatible with that advocated by Dunn (1988) and Tizard and Hughes (1984). They have argued for the need to study development within the emotional context of the family and to assess children's competencies in environments which are meaningful to them.
   Observation sessions were scheduled for weekday mornings or afternoons. Mothers were present throughout the observation sessions but did not constantly interact with the target child because of other demands on their time. Other family members were present inconsistently (see chapter 4). The observer used a portable videorecorder to make a continuous recording of the target child's activities. She did not attempt to elicit particular behaviors or to structure the situation in any way.
   The advantage of naturalistic observations is that they are more likely than assessments conducted in unfamiliar contexts to capture children's newly emerging abilities, and hence are less likely to underestimate children's competence. For example, in the context of her own bedroom, and in the company of her sister, three-year-old Molly's pretending is surprisingly complex in structure, function, and theme. Molly and Rachael not only communicate a series of specific symbolic transformations (e.g., "I'm a doggie," "I'm a baby doggie," "You are a cheese cracker that I

bite"), but this pretend talk apparently functions to justify aggression arising from a seemingly unresolvable conflict occurring outside of the pretend frame.

Longitudinal design. The study entailed seven successive longitudinal samples of behavior during the period from one to four years of age (with data points at twelve, sixteen, twenty, twenty-four, thirty, thirty-six, and forty-eight months of age). This period spans the emergence of the first fleeting pretend gestures through the development of elaborate pretend scenarios. The findings reported in this book are based on observations at twelve, twenty-four, thirty-six, and forty-eight months of age for a total of 116.5 hours of observation.

While many fine studies document children's early play through cross-sectional (e.g., Dunn and Wooding 1977; Kavanaugh, Whittington and Cerbone 1983) or short range longitudinal designs (e.g., Sachs 1980), there are few longitudinal studies encompassing three full years of development for the same children (but see Wolfe, Rygh and Altshuler 1984). Our design allows us to juxtapose stable individual differences with normative patterns of developmental change. For example, from the age of twenty-four months, Molly engaged in highly verbal, imaginative role play involving dolls. Moreover, her keen interest in Rachael's Tropical Skipper doll at thirty-six months was evident one year later at forty-eight months.

Extended observation sessions. While most studies of pretending involve brief (a few minutes to one hour) samples of play from a relatively large number of children, we chose instead to obtain lengthy (three to four hours) samples of play from a relatively small number of children. Table 2.1 shows the length of each observation session. One important advantage of this strategy is that it provides exceptionally in-depth coverage of each child's pretending. A second advantage is that we were able to capture even prolonged pretend episodes in their entirety as well as sequences of related episodes, thereby permitting analysis of the mundane contexts from which pretending emerges, who initiated the episodes, and how they were

Table 2.1.
Total time observed in hours for each child

	12 mos	24 mos	36 mos	48 mos	TOTAL
	(N=8)	(N=9)	(N=9)	(N=9)	(N=9)
Charlie[a]	1.6	3.6	4.2	3.4	12.8
Elizabeth	3.2	4.0	3.2	2.9	13.3
Justin	3.6	3.8	3.8	3.7	14.9
John	3.8	3.9	3.1	3.1	13.9
Joe	1.8	3.6	3.7	3.3	12.4
Kathy	2.0	2.3	3.2	3.4	10.9
Molly	2.5	3.9	4.2	3.6	14.2
Michael	—[b]	3.5	3.5	3.3	10.3
Nancy	3.1	3.2	3.9	3.6	13.8
Total	**21.6**	**31.8**	**32.8**	**30.3**	**116.5**

[a] Pseudonyms are used throughout this report.
[b] The first observation of Michael occurred at sixteen months.

sustained. Furthermore, our findings suggest that extended observations provide a more accurate picture of pretending than can be achieved through brief observations (see chapter 6). At thirty-six and forty-eight months of age, the most extended and complex episodes of pretending occurred subsequent to the first hour of observation. For example, the pretend episode excerpted at the beginning of this chapter was one of seven related episodes, totalling more than twelve minutes, that Molly and Rachael engaged in during the third hour of observation. All revolved around conflict over the possession of Tropical Skipper.

Fortuitously double blind. In addition to these features of our research strategy, there are other features that speak to a methodological issue of perennial concern in observational studies: how to minimize the effects of the observation procedures on the findings? Especially relevant to this issue is the fact that our study was fortuitously "double blind": the data were originally collected for a study of vocabulary development, and hence neither the observer nor the parent was aware that pretending would be the focus of inquiry. (Mothers subsequently granted their permission for the study of pretend play.) This makes it unlikely that the mothers consciously or unconsciously altered their pretend behaviors per se in response to being observed. Similarly, it is unlikely that the observer inadvertently encouraged pretending. In addition, since the children and their mothers were not recruited with the intention of studying pretend play, it is unlikely that their pretend play was different from that of other members of their community. And, indeed, the children reached the major milestones of pretending at the usual ages, i.e., pretending was barely established at twelve months, children's first explicit role transformations appeared at approximately thirty-six months, and children began to sustain pretend play with other children during the fourth year of life.

Rapport building. Although mothers and children did not know that pretend play was to be a focus of study, they obviously knew that they were being observed. It was therefore extremely important that the families felt comfortable with the observer. Prior to each observation session the observer visited informally with the mothers and children in an attempt to establish and maintain rapport. The mothers and observer talked about their families, professional and other common interests, current events, etc. The children were mostly interested in examining and operating the video camera. During the actual observation, the observer attempted to remain as unobtrusive as possible. Mothers were instructed to go about their usual routines and to ignore the observer as much as possible. Further discussion of the impact of the observation procedures is provided in chapter 4.

In sum, nine young children from affluent, highly educated families were studied repeatedly during the period in which pretend play emerges and rapidly develops. They were observed in their homes as they went about their ordinary activities, with mothers and other family members near at hand.

Observation sessions were lengthy enough to permit analysis of entire episodes of pretending as they emerged and unfolded. This research strategy, while atypical in developmental studies of pretending, is appropriate to our goal of investigating everyday pretending in an ecologically valid manner.

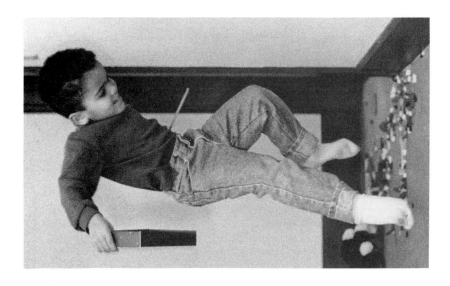

3

How Much Do Children Pretend?

Four-year-old Kathy and her nine-year-old sister, Susan, are playing in the living room. Kathy is grooming a small toy pony named North Star while Susan is engrossed in the adventures of her Barbie doll, Superhair, who is attending an imaginary school. Suddenly, North Star becomes lost in a dark cave (under sofa cushions) and calls out for help to Superhair. Kathy, talking for North Star, says excitedly, "Get me out of here! See all the doors—" Susan answers, talking for Superhair, "Does Kathy know where you are?" North Star begins whimpering and frantically walking around in circles, "No! There are about—thirty dragons in—no not thirty! About one hundred!" Superhair calmly replies, "Well, find one with purple spots."

The now highly distraught North Star begins moaning and breathing rapidly, "No! There are one hundred dragons in this place. Even there are monsters! This is— Oh! Oh! I can't wait!" Superhair, speaking with exaggerated calm: "Well, try to make the biggest dragon of them all scare the rest away. Now, try to find one that's growing." North Star (more fast breathing): "All right I already found one that's eating. That makes him grow. Oh!!" Superhair: "So is there one eating and growing that has purple spots?" North Star, still pacing: "Well, no! They all don't have spots. They're like real black dragons and they—" Superhair: "Well, try to make one go forward . . . "

North Star: "OK. But who's that dragon?" Superhair: "It's stepping forward right now and it's got purple spots." North Star: "I don't know who that is. Who is it?" Superhair: "It might call itself, 'Lick.' . . . " North Star: "But I can't seem to find one with purple spots that's going forward. . . . " Superhair: "Well I'll make one fly. All right? And that'll be Lick. . . . All right. Lick is flying."

Kathy steps out of role momentarily to correct Susan's rendition: "Not yet. I didn't try my dragon power. OK?" She continues, chanting, "Powers of light make these dragons fly away nice. Ahhhhhhh!" Susan: "Are they doing it?" Kathy: "Uhhuh. . . . It's working. . . . " The crisis resolved, Susan returns to her imaginary school, and Kathy to grooming her pony.

* * *

This example is excerpted from a forty-five-minute episode in which the two sisters brought their dolls to life and transformed the living room into a dark and frightening cave filled with flying dragons. Although Kathy was not one of the most frequent pretenders in our sample, she devoted fifty-two minutes to pretend activity during the fourth observation session, most of it revolving around North Star and Superhair.

The belief that pretending has a salutary effect on development, as well as specific theoretical claims about the role of play in development, rest on the assumption that pretending is a major occupation of young children. The literature, however, contains few clues to the actual amount of time that young children spend pretending. Piaget (1962) described pretend play as infrequent and brief during the second year of life, increasing in frequency during the next three or four years. Subsequent empirical research indicates that pretend play first appears at about one year of age (e.g., Fenson et al. 1976; Rosenblatt 1977; Fein and Apfel 1979), and increases in proportion relative to other types of play from approximately two to six years (e.g., Manwell and Mengert 1934; Sanders and Harper 1976; Emmerich 1977; Hetherington, Cox and Cox 1979; Sachs, Goldman, and Chaille 1985; for review, see Rubin, Fein, and Vandenberg 1983). Miller and Garvey (1984) report that 11 to 20 percent of the intelligible utterances of two year olds at home occurred during mother-baby role play. Dunn and Dale (1984) report that during unstructured home observations of two year olds, pretend play filled 21 percent of the time. There have been few other attempts to estimate exactly how frequently children pretend.

In addition to examining the overall frequency of pretending, it is important to consider the length of individual episodes of play. Although the overall frequency of pretending may reflect children's propensities to pretend, the duration of individual episodes of pretend play may reflect the players' abilities to sustain and elaborate the play. Indeed, Fiese (1987) found a positive relation between the duration of episodes of pretend play and their level of symbolic maturity. Existing studies, however, have not investigated relationships between developmental changes in the overall frequency of pretending and developmental changes in the duration of individual episodes. If the overall amount of play increases with children's age, but the duration of the episodes remains stable, then the increase in frequency may only reflect an increasing disposition to play and not an increasing facility with play. If children become more skilled at pretending, then a developmental increase should be apparent in the duration of episodes. In this study, we found marked developmental increases not only in the overall frequency of pretending, but in the mean duration of children's episodes of pretend play as well.

Defining and Identifying Episodes of Pretend Play

Answering these simple questions—How much do children pretend? How sustained are episodes of pretending?—necessarily involves confronting all the complexities of defining and quantifying pretend play. Following Garvey (1990), we defined pretend play as a subcategory of play in which actions, objects, persons, places, or other aspects of the here and now are transformed or treated nonliterally. For example, a superstar doll or a stuffed animal is animated; a sibling is transformed into a cheese cracker; behaviors conventionally associated with one context are enacted in a different context (e.g. a child says "nighty-night," lies down on the kitchen floor, and covers up with a napkin). Pretend play includes fleeting enactments, such as putting a cup to a doll's mouth and saying, "mm good," and lengthy, narrativelike sequences such as Kathy's adventures with North Star and Superhair. It sometimes incorporates construction play with blocks and Lego building sets; repetitive ritual play (see Garvey 1990); and scenarios that occurred in the past. Actions that were suggested by a replica object's unique and salient physical properties (e.g., placing a toy biscuit in a toy bowl) had to be accompanied by other verbal and nonverbal actions (e.g., using a toy spoon to "eat" the biscuit) to be counted as pretense. Otherwise such actions were excluded on the grounds that they were ambiguous as to whether the child was treating the object nonliterally (see Rocissano 1982). Further description of pretend play are provided in appendix A.

Ambiguous activities that are excluded from our pretend play category are discussed in appendix B.

We defined an episode of pretend play as a continuous stretch of pretending on a given theme or topic. Episodes usually involved both verbal and nonverbal enactment, but episodes that were exclusively nonverbal or exclusively verbal also were included. Episodes began with the first action of pretend play produced by or directed at the child. For example, thirty-month-old Nancy picked up and visually examined the contents of a box containing the parts of a replica hamburger, e.g., a plastic bun, pattie, onion, pickle, etc. Then she placed the pickle to her lips and gestured as if eating. The episode began with this first gesture of eating. Episodes continued as long as the chain of transformational actions and supporting responses continued and ended with the final action of play produced by or directed at the child.

In the interests of establishing a conservative estimate of the amount of time that the children spent pretending, we applied two additional criteria to the transcribed episodes. First, to be credited with an episode of pretend play, the target child had to produce at least one spontaneous transformation within the episode. That is, if the child's only contribution to an episode consisted of an imitation of another player's transformation, that episode was not included as pretend play for the child. For example, twelve-month-old Nancy's mother animated a Fisher-Price train with "Toot-toot-toot." Subsequently, twelve-month-old Nancy picked up the toy and said, "Toot-toot," but provided no further transformations. Nancy was not credited with pretend play, although her mother was credited with directing pretend play to Nancy. Similarly, if the child's only contribution to an episode consisted of carrying out a pretend action suggested by the mother, that episode was not credited to the child.

Second, we took into account brief forays out of the pretend mode. Sometimes, in the midst of an episode, the child momentarily moved into a nonpretend activity. Time intervals of less than one minute encompassing only literal or ambiguous actions within episodes were considered "digressions" and were subtracted in computing the total time of the episode. For example, thirty-month-old Charlie and his mother were engaged in an episode of mother-baby role play when a fire engine sounded outside the open window. They briefly commented on the siren and then continued the play. This fifteen-second digression was subtracted in computing the total time of the episode. Pretending that was interrupted for more than one minute was treated as two episodes. For example, thirty-six-month-old Nancy announced that she was a cowboy and proceeded to plan the scenario with her mother. Distracted, she attempted to put on her shoe for approximately two and one-half minutes. Then she mounted and ordered her stick horse, "giddeyup." The first episode began with Nancy's proclamation, "I'm a cowboy," and ended with her first action on her shoe. The second episode began when she mounted her horse.[1]

Transcription

All episodes of pretending were transcribed in full from each videotape. The transcript included a verbatim record of verbal behaviors, a detailed description of nonverbal behaviors, and additional contextual information concerning the time and location of the play as well as the objects that were used.

Intercoder Reliabilities

Intercoder reliabilities were obtained following training using portions of the actual videotapes and transcripts. Data used for the reliability checks were randomly chosen, excluding data used for training. Two coders independently viewed and coded 20 percent of the data at each age level for each child. One of the raters was naive as to the hypotheses.

A two-step procedure was followed in estimating intercoder reliability for identification of pretend episodes. (See table 3.1.) First, the degree to which episodes of pretend play could be accurately identified from videotape was assessed. Percentage of agreement was 91 percent, with a range from 87 percent at thirty-six months to 92 percent at twelve and twenty-four months.

Table 3.1.
Intercoder reliabilities for identifying pretend episodes:
Percentage agreement

Code	12 mos	24 mos	36 mos	48 mos
Episodes of pretending[b]	92 (13)[a]	92 (37)	87 (37)	91 (34)
Beginnings of episodes[c]	100 (10)	100 (27)	90 (31)	97 (32)
Endings of episodes[c]	92 (10)	93 (27)	84 (31)	94 (32)
Digressions[c]	1.0 (4)	.84 (34)	.82 (16)	.81 (55)

[a] Base figures used to compute reliabilities.
[b] Based on all episodes identified from videotapes by one or both raters during 20 percent of the total time of each observation at each age level for each child.
[c] Based on 20 percent of episodes for each child at each age level.

A second reliability check was conducted on written transcripts. These transcripts were especially prepared to include both the episode itself and a segment of behaviors preceding and following the episode. The segments on either side of the episode amounted to one minute's worth of videotape each, yielding varying amounts of transcript. The coders independently identified the beginnings and endings of the episodes. Percentage of agreement for the beginnings of episodes was 96 percent, with a range from 90 percent at thirty-six months to 100 percent at twelve and twenty-four months. Percentage of agreement for the endings of episodes was 90 percent, with a range from 84 percent at thirty-six months to 94 percent at forty-eight months. Percentage of agreement for identifying digressions was also assessed from these transcripts and ranged from 81 percent at forty-eight months to 100 percent at twelve months with an overall value of 83 percent.

Results

How Much Do Children Pretend?

The amount of time that the children pretended is displayed in table 3.2. Overall, summing across children and across ages, the children pretended for a total of twelve hours or 11 percent of the total observation time (116.5 hours). The children pretended as little as 4 percent (John) of the time and as much as 15 percent (Joe).

Half of the children observed at twelve months engaged in pretend play, but the amount of pretending was extremely brief, amounting to a total of 1.3 minutes. By twenty-four

Table 3.2.
Total minutes of child pretend play[a]

	12 mos	24 mos	36 mos	48 mos	TOTAL
	(N=8)	(N=9)	(N=9)	(N=9)	(N=9)
Charlie	0	2.7	69.5	19.8	92.0
Elizabeth	1.0	20.9	6.7	45.1	73.7
Justin	0	6.9	59.0	11.4	77.3
John	0.1	18.9	18.7	0.3	38.0
Joe	0	29.0	33.0	51.7	113.7
Kathy	0.1	1.6	15.8	51.7	69.2
Molly	0	18.5	26.6	58.5	103.6
Michael	—[b]	4.3	6.9	59.4	70.6
Nancy	0.1	6.3	30.7	46.1	83.2
TOTAL	**1.3**	**109.1**	**266.9**	**344.0**	**721.3**
	(.02 hrs.)	(1.8 hrs.)	(4.5 hrs.)	(5.7 hrs.)	(12.0 hrs.)

[a] Recall that each child was observed for approximately 3 to 4 hours at each data point for a total sample of 10.3 to 14.9 hours per child for an overall total of 116.5 hours of observation.

[b] The first observation of Michael occurred at sixteen months.

months, all children pretended, and four of the children engaged in pretend play for more than fifteen minutes. At thirty-
six months, two of the nine children pretended for less than
fifteen minutes and four pretended for more than thirty minutes. At forty-eight months, two of the children pretended for
less than fifteen minutes, and six pretended for more than
forty-five minutes.

Because observation times varied somewhat across the observation sessions, we converted the amount of pretend play
into rate measures. Two measures of pretend play were employed: "minutes per hour" and "minutes per episode." Minutes per hour is the total duration of all episodes, excluding

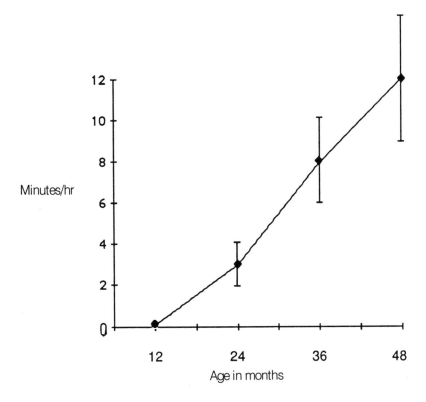

Figure 3.1. The mean frequency and SEM[a] of children's
pretend play from 12 to 14 months.

[a] SEM = Standard error of the mean

digressions, divided by the total hours of observation. Minutes per episodes (or "duration") is the total minutes of pretending divided by the total number of episodes.

As figure 3.1 indicates, there was an increase in the rate of pretending across the age range from a mean of 0.06 minutes per hour at twelve months, to 3.3. at twenty-four months, 7.8 at thirty-six months, and 12.4 at forty-eight months. This pattern of steady increase held not only on average: it applied to five of the individual children, with one data point departing from the pattern for each of the four other children. (A repeated measures ANOVA performed on the rate of pretend play revealed a main effect of age [F (3, 23) = 9.01, p < 0.0001].)

How Sustained Are Episodes of Pretend Play?

As figure 3.2 summarizes, the mean duration of pretend play episodes increased dramatically across the age range from 0.2 minutes per episode at twelve months, to 0.9 at twenty-four

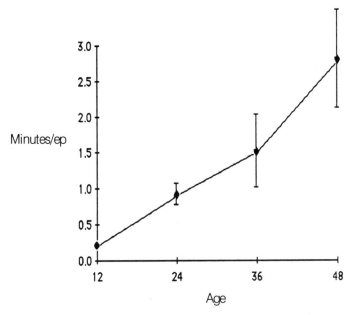

Figure 3.2. The mean minutes and SEM of pretend play per episode from 12 to 48 months.

months, 1.5 at thirty-six months, and 2.8 at forty-eight months. There was relatively little individual variation in this pattern: all children observed at twelve months showed an increase in the mean duration of pretend episodes at twenty-four months; seven showed an increase from twenty-four to thirty-six months; and six showed an increase from thirty-six to forty-eight months. (A repeated measures ANOVA performed on the duration of pretend play episodes revealed a main effect of age [F (3, 19) = 4.08, $p < .03$].)

Discussion

Procedures for assessing how much children pretend were developed and applied to the recorded observations of the children as they went about their ordinary activities in and around the home. During our observations, pretend play was a relatively frequent activity that increased steadily in frequency and duration as the children grew from twelve to forty-eight months. Although children varied in the extent to which they engaged in pretend play, there was relatively little individual variation in their tendency to engage in more pretending and more sustained pretending as they got older.

These findings are consistent with previous findings that pretend play first appears in brief, rare episodes at about one year of age (see Rubin, Fein, and Vandenberg 1983, for review), and thereby suggest that our sample of pretenders is not unusual. In addition, this long-range longitudinal study of pretending in the home corroborates Piaget's observation that pretend play increases in frequency during the preschool years. But most importantly, the study revealed that these young children spent a significant amount of their daily lives pretending. Our observations occurred during weekday mornings or afternoons. We estimate that during the period from 8 A.M. to 5 P.M. these children spent on average about half an hour pretending at twenty-four months, more than one hour at thirty-six months, and approximately two hours at forty-eight months. Unfortunately, it is not possible to compare these estimates to a cross-cultural literature; to our

knowledge there are no comparable studies of how much pretending occurs on a daily basis in other cultural groups. Although claims have been made that children from other
cultures, including children from lower SES groups in Western societies, engage in little pretend play, both Rubin, Fein,
and Vandenberg (1983) and Schwartzman (1978) conclude
that there is insufficient evidence to support such claims. In
the next chapter we shall see that within the community we
studied, pretending was not only frequent but was also so-
cially conducted.

Notes

1. Note that verbal digressions are not excluded if they are
   accompanied by clear gestures of enactment. For example, thirty-six-month-old Nancy was pretending to
   drive a car with her mother. During the episode her
   mother initiated a discussion of past actions actually
   performed by the child's father while driving. Nancy
   participated in the discussion while continuing to enact
   steering the car and making occasional sound effects.
   Because the literal talk was accompanied by clear pretend play, this portion of the episode was not excluded
   as a digression for the child. In contrast, thirty-six-
   month-old Nancy and her mother established that bat-
   ting a balloon back and forth represented a "soccer
   game." They continued to rally the balloon while discussing their upcoming Halloween party. Unlike the
   actions of steering a make-believe car to accompanying
   sound effects, however, the actions of hitting the balloon became ambiguous when accompanied by such
   literal talk and were considered digressions: were the
   players still engaged in a pretend soccer game or a new
   episode of physical play?

4

The Interpersonal Context of
Everyday Pretending

Example 1: Joe at twelve months Joe toddles towards a large cardboard box filling up most of the dining room. He vocalizes. Mother: "Oh, you want to go in your house? Oh, you can't find the door!" (The "door" is a hole covered by a cardboard flap.) "Where's your new house? Where's the door? See if you can find the door. Here's the door over here." She indicates the door and Joe crawls in the house, vocalizing. "Yea! You are in it!"

Example 2: Joe at forty-eight months Joe and his mother are in the kitchen. Joe screams loudly and runs across the room holding up his clenched fist. Joe: "My birdie gonna fly up over . . .!" He screams again. His mother asks with exaggerated concern: "What was that noise? What happened? What's that noise?" Joe screams again. Mother: "Joe, what's happening to your birdie?" Joe continues to make noises as he "flies" his "bird" across the room to his mother, "An alligator caught it!" Mother: "Ah! Oh!" Joe screams some more and makes chewing sound effects as he runs through the kitchen making a glove eat the imaginary bird. Joe: "An alligator caught it!" Joe growls at his mother with the glove. Mother: "Oh, a big alligator!" Joe growls, "I'm a big alligator!", and then growls again. His mother holds up a clenched hand: "I'm a bigger alligator than you and I'm gonna catch you!" Joe screams, growls some more and then gets down on his hands and knees and jumps like a frog, "Ribbet!"

* * *

During the three years in which we observed Joe, we saw him pretend alone only occasionally. Most of the time he pretended with his mother, who, as primary caregiver in the family, was the person most consistently available to him. From the age of twelve months, before we observed him produce pretend play, his mother encouraged his pretend play by providing materials and making suggestions. Even at the age of four years, when Joe was a highly skilled pretender capable of sustaining pretend play on his own or with his brother, he sought his mother's participation. Our observations of Joe raise questions about the social origins of pretending, questions about which theorists disagree. We begin this chapter with a discussion of this controversy. We derive several specific questions which are addressed later in this chapter and in the two succeeding chapters.

Theoretical Perspectives on the Social Origins of Pretend Play

According to the prevailing Piagetian view, symbolic play arises spontaneously from the structure of individual thought and not until several years later does it become sufficiently "socialized" to permit symbols to be shared (i.e., collective symbolism). Piaget's (1962) otherwise meticulous observations of children's initial forays into pretending omit information about the interpersonal context of pretending, with the implication that symbolic play would develop regardless of whether anyone pretended with the child. Given this characterization of early pretending it is not surprising that there has been little systematic empirical investigation of its social context. In an important review article, Fein asserted, "It is unlikely that parents play pretend games with their young children or model such games . . . ." (1981, p. 1106).

Recently, however, several researchers have challenged this view, citing evidence that many caregivers in Western middle-class communities do pretend with young children, and suggesting that such interactions facilitate the emergence and early elaboration of pretend play (e.g., Dunn 1986; Dunn and Dale 1984; Garvey 1990). Mothers are not only responsive to young children's pretending but the form of their responses changes as children become more proficient players (Kavanaugh, Whittington, Cerbone 1983; Miller and Garvey 1984; Sachs 1980). In addition, toddlers' pretend play with caregivers is more sustained (Dunn and Wooding 1977; Slade 1987), complex (Fiese 1987; Slade 1987), and diverse (O'Connell and Bretherton 1984) than their solo pretending.

These findings raise the possibility that mothers' participation does affect the development of everyday pretending.

There are several routes by which such influence could proceed. First, caregivers' infectious enthusiasm for pretending
and their creation of an encouraging climate for play may
ignite the child's interest. Singer and Singer (1990) argue that
there must be a key person in the child's life who inspires and
sanctions play and accepts the child's inventions with respect
and delight. They examined the autobiographies and biogra-
phies of famous writers, artists, and scientists. In many of these
accounts a mother, father, older sibling, governess, friend,
cousin, aunt, uncle, or teacher was mentioned repeatedly in
discussions of childhood fantasy. Anton Chekov believed that
he derived his talent from his father and his soul from his
mother who, despite the burden of raising six children, fos-
tered his love of make-believe. In his autobiography, A. A.
Milne credits the "unforgettable memories" of his childhood
and the parents who sanctioned his play as crucial elements in
his creation of an imaginary forest with its famous inhabitant,
Winnie the Pooh.

Classic developmental theories of symbol formation suggest another way by which caregivers contribute to the development of pretending, namely by providing the interpersonal
context in which symbolic competencies emerge. According to
Werner and Kaplan (1963), symbolic activity originates in an
intimate interpersonal context of mother-child interaction. In
the course of development, the interpersonal distance between
child and addressee widens, and the symbolic vehicle becomes
more autonomous and hence more widely shareable. The psychoanalytic view is similar in that symbolic activity is seen as
originating within the mother-child relationship. According to
Winnicott (1971), the infant's capacity to create living symbols
(e.g., transitional objects) develops within a sequence of changing relationships with the mother. In this view, what is crucial
for healthy development is the mother's capacity to accept the
child's creative activities, fitting in with his or her play activities before introducing her own ideas into the play.

A third way in which parents may support their children's
pretending is through socializing them into the conventions
and competencies necessary to pretend within a given community. The strongest view of caregivers'contribution to early

pretending was articulated by El'Konin (1966). (See also Smolucha 1989, 1991.) Influenced by Vygotsky's sociohistorical theory of intellectual development, he argued that children are socialized into pretending through language-mediated interactions with adults. He cites numerous examples in which a toddler's renaming of an object was traceable to an earlier episode in which an adult introduced the renaming or in which a child's adoption of a pretend role was suggested by an adult. Indeed, he claims that some sort of adult modelling is necessary for the emergence of pretend play. In parallel with Vygotsky's (1962) view that speech develops from the social to the private, and in opposition to Piaget's (1962) position, El'Konin (1966) views pretend play as developing from the interpersonal to the intrapersonal.

El'Konin's idea that caregivers socialize children into pretending through particular kinds of communications is echoed in recent accounts that take a communicative view of pretending (Garvey 1990; Miller and Garvey 1984; Garvey and Kramer, 1989). These accounts emphasize that coordinating a pretend performance with a partner depends heavily upon specific social/communicative conventions and that these conventions are acquired in the context of play interactions with more experienced partners. Still other contemporary theorists take a compatible position while also emphasizing the child's active role in acquiring skills. Rogoff (1990) argues that children actively appropriate skills through their guided participation as apprentices in culturally valued activities. Similarly, O'Connell and Bretherton (1984) stress that pretending is reciprocally driven by adult and child with the child actively selecting from the information provided. From these perspectives, it is important to understand both what caregivers do in their pretend interactions with children and how children's pretend activity is or is not affected.

The foregoing discussion raises several basic empirical questions about the social nature of everyday pretending. What is its interpersonal context? How is social pretense conducted? Are episodes of pretend play affected by a partner's participation? These questions are obviously related, but they are analytically separable and will be taken up in turn. The interpersonal context will be addressed in this chapter, the social conduct of pretending and the outcomes of mothers' participation in the pretend episode will be addressed in chapters 5 and 6, respectively.

The Interpersonal Context of Early Pretending

Is early pretense a social activity or is it conducted alone, as implied by Piaget and assumed by most subsequent researchers? If early pretend play is social, this would be consistent with the possibility that other people affect its development. Several naturalistic, longitudinal studies suggest that pretend play may be social from its inception. Wolfe (1982) and Beizer (1991) cite examples of the unskilled attempts of children aged ten to eighteen months to involve others in their earliest pretend play. In Dale's (1983) study of second-born twenty-four-month-olds, 59 percent of pretend play episodes included some participation by mother and/or sibling. Dunn (1986) reports that the time young children spent in joint pretend play with mothers or siblings was far greater than the time spent in solitary pretend play.

Verification of these findings would raise a further issue, namely, who are children's play partners? Children could benefit in different ways from pretending with different sorts of partners. Indeed, Dunn and Dale (1984) suggest that mothers and siblings participate differently in children's early pretending. Mothers acted as spectators, offering pretend suggestions and comments, whereas siblings entered the joint pretense as "complementary actors," who performed pretend actions and adopted pretend identities.

If mothers are major play partners for their toddlers, then it is important to consider when such interactions begin relative to the inception of children's pretending. Pretend play emerges at roughly one year of age (Rubin, Fein, and Vandenberg 1983), and there is some evidence that parents direct pretend play to children at this age (Kavanaugh, Whittington, and Cerbone 1983; Crawley and Sherrod 1984; Beizer 1991), but no studies have examined whether mothers introduce pretending prior to or after the emergence of pretending in their children. If mothers do direct pretend play to young children who are not yet capable of pretending, or who are just beginning to pretend, this could provide children with models on which to base their own initial forays into pretending.

Behavioral Codes

In order to answer these questions, our first step was to define what we meant by social. Pretend play was considered to be social when the child directed pretend play to another person or, subsequent to or immediately prior to producing a transformational action or statement, attended to the pretend play directed to him or her by another person. Transformational actions or statements could be directed at the other verbally (e.g. addressing the other by name), or nonverbally by directing an action towards the other. For example, thirty-six-month-old Nancy and her mother were credited with social pretending as they animated mittens with kitten faces sewn on them. Nancy's mother made her mitten greet Nancy's mitten, "Hi, friend." Nancy made her mitten reply, "Hi. How are you?"

Note that by this definition the mere presence of another person does not constitute social pretending: if the other was not actively involved in the pretense, the play was regarded as solo. For example, Nancy's enactment of piano playing at twenty-four months was considered solo as she lifted her fingers up and down on the table and sang, "Ahhhhhhhh. Ehhhhhhhhh." Her mother was present and even inquired, "Are you playing the piano?" but Nancy did not respond. She simply continued her initial actions.

Note also that a single episode of pretending could contain both social and solo portions, and only the social portions were considered when computing the percentage of pretend play time that was social. For example, thirty-six-month-old Molly joined five-year-old Rachael's Barbie doll play. She chose a doll and briefly enacted "walking in mud" with Rachael (social pretend play). Then, each child independently pursued the grooming of her doll (solo pretend play). Finally, both children collaborated to enact "going to school" with their dolls (social pretend play).

Intercoder Reliability

Coding was done from written transcripts. Intercoder reliabilities for time spent in social pretending were obtained from portions of the actual transcripts following training. Agreement between two independent raters coding 20 percent of the data was 100 percent at twelve months, and 91 percent at the subsequent ages. Data used for the reliability checks were randomly chosen from each child at each age level excluding data used for training. One of the raters was naive as to the hypotheses.

Results[1]

Is Children's Early Pretend Play Primarily Social or Solo?

Figure 4.1 shows that pretend play was predominantly social across the entire age span, ranging from a mean of 68 to 75 percentage of children's total pretend play time. A repeated measures ANOVA revealed no significant changes from twelve to forty-eight months in the mean percentage of pretending that involved a partner. (The F statistic was computed with age x child as the error term.)

The pattern of predominantly social pretending held not only on average, but across the individual children as well. The majority of pretend play time was social at every sampled age level for five children, and at three of the four age levels for two children. Only Charlie and Michael showed a preponderance of solo pretending: they each had a low percentage of social pretending at two of the age levels. Of the six samples in which solo pretend play predominated, four occurred at the later age levels (Charlie thirty-six months, Michael thirty-six months, Michael forty-eight months, Justin forty-eight months). These data thus provide no support for the notion that pretend play develops from a solo to a social activity.

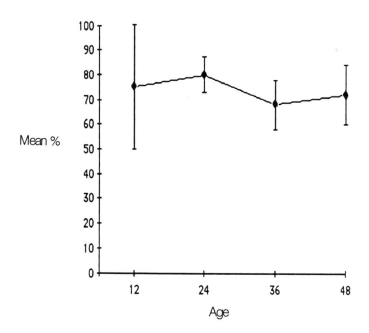

Figure 4.1 The mean percentage and SEM of pretend play that is social from 12 to 48 months.

With Whom Do Children Pretend?

As figure 4.2 shows, mothers were children's major play partners through thirty-six months; at forty-eight months children played about equally with mothers and other children (i.e., siblings and other child playmates). An Age by Partner (i.e., mother vs. other children) repeated measures ANOVA performed on the mean percentage of children's social pretend play time revealed a main effect of partner, F (1, 50) = 9.16, p < 0.01, but not age, and a significant age by partner interaction, F (2, 50) = 4.76, p < 0.01.

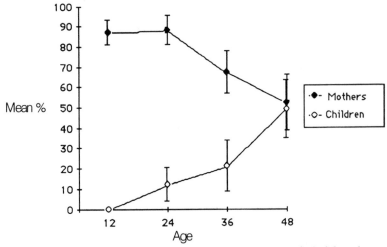

Figure 4.2 The mean percentage and SEM[a] of children's social pretend play time involving mothers and other children as play partners from 12 to 48 months.

[a]SEM=Standard error of the mean.

There was little individual variation in the tendency for mothers to be the primary play partner. At twenty-four months there was remarkable consistency across the children: social pretending occurred exclusively with mothers for five of the children and primarily with mothers (0.73 to 0.95 of social pretend time) for another three children. The remaining child pretended primarily with another adult. Mothers were the primary pretend play partners for six of the nine children at thirty-six months, but for only three of the nine children at forty-eight months.

There was some individual variation in developmental trends. Five of the children showed a clear decline from twenty-four to forty- eight months in the percentage of time spent pretending with their mothers. Correspondingly, these same five children showed an increase over the same period in the time spent pretending with other children so that by forty-eight months 54 to 100 percent of their social pretending involved another child. All of these children had siblings, and four had older siblings. Of the remaining four children, three had limited, if any, opportunity to play with other children. Although the remaining child had an older sibling who was present during the taping sessions, there was considerable conflict between the siblings during the observations and the focal child pretended primarily with his mother during all the observation sessions.

The question arises as to whether the finding that mothers were children's primary play partners until forty-eight months reflects their preference for mothers over other children as play partners, or whether it simply reflects a family ecology in which children have much greater opportunity to pretend with their mothers. A definitive answer to this question must await future studies designed to permit equal access to mothers and other children, and to differentiate between older siblings, younger siblings and friends. However, further examination of the current data set does provide preliminary clues as to the relative contribution of availability vs. preference for different play partners. As expected, the social ecology in these families was such that mothers were consistently present during the observation sessions, fathers were rarely present, and other children were inconsistently present. Across the entire age range, approximately half of the focal children had access to other children for a substantial portion of the observation session. At twelve months, four children had access to other children for a mean of 30 percent (± 13 percent) of the total observation sessions. At twenty-four months, four children had access to other children for a mean of 31 percent (± 14 percent) of the total observation sessions. At thirty-six months, five children had access to other children for a mean of 32 percent (± 14 percent) of the total observation sessions. At forty-eight months, four children had access to other children for a mean of

44 percent (± 18 percent) of the total observation sessions. Of those children who did have access to other children, zero of four pretended with them at twelve months, two of four at twenty-four months, three of five at thirty- six months, and four of four at forty-eight months. These preliminary findings suggest that while children had many more opportunities to pretend with their mothers than with other children throughout the entire age range, at the younger ages they took little advantage of opportunities to pretend with other children.

When Do Mothers Begin to Pretend with Their Children Relative to the Inception of Pretend Play in Their Children?

As table 4.1 illustrates, of the eight children who were observed at twelve months, only four produced any pretending and their pretending occurred very infrequently. At this same age, however, all eight mothers produced some pretend play directed to and attended to by their children. Indeed, all but one of the individual mothers produced pretending at a higher rate than did her child. In contrast, by twenty-four months, all nine children and nine mothers produced pretend

---

Table 4.1.

The mean frequency and SEM of child and mother pretending from 12 to 48 months in minutes per hour

	Age in months							
	12		**24**		**36**		**48**	
	Child	Mother	Child	Mother	Child	Mother	Child	Mother
Mean	0.10	0.40	3.00	2.00	8.00	3.00	12.00	3.00
SEM	0.04	0.10	1.00	1.00	2.00	1.00	3.00	1.00
N[a]	4	8	9	9	9	9	9	9

[a] The total number of mothers and children pretending.

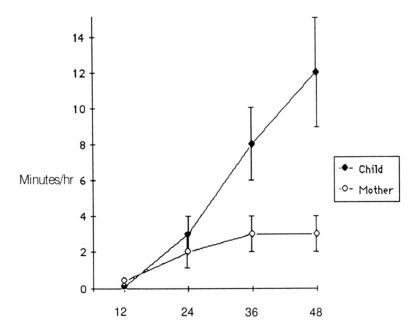

Figure 4.3 The mean frequency and SEM of child and mother pretending from 12 to 48 months in minutes per hour

[a]Note: On this and all other figures, errors bars are included only when they are larger than the symbol indicating mean amount of play.

play and they did so at about equal rates. Note that caregiver pretend play was considered only if the child was clearly attending to the pretending (observing or vocalizing) and hence is a conservative estimate of how much pretending caregivers actually directed to children.

Overall, children produced more pretend play than mothers, and pretending increased over the age range. (See figure 4.3) The rate of children's pretend play increased dramatically over the age range, but mothers' pretending only increased from twelve to twenty-four months and then remained relatively stable. (See table 4.1) An Age by Player (i.e., mother and target child) repeated measures ANOVA performed on the rate of pretend play revealed a main effect of age, F (3, 23) 7.08, p < 0.001, and player, F (1, 23) = 8.78, p < 0.01. There also was a significant Age by Player interaction, F (3, 23) = 2.99, p < 0.05.

Although all individual mothers and children increased their rates of pretending from twelve to twenty-four months and all but one child increased dramatically in rates of pretending from twenty- four to forty-eight months, there were individual differences as to whether mothers increased or decreased in their rates of pretending from twenty-four to forty-eight months. All individual children produced more pretending than their mothers at thirty-six and forty-eight months.

Discussion

Our investigation of the social context of pretend play revealed that everyday pretending occurred predominantly in interaction with others during the entire period of emergence and early development. For these offspring of affluent, highly educated parents, pretend play was social from its inception, with mothers serving as children's primary play partners. In the context of their own homes, all mothers directed pretend play to their children at twelve months of age, although pretend play had emerged barely in some children and not at all in others. Mothers remained the primary play partners through thirty-six months; at forty-eight months the children pretended roughly equally with mothers and other children.

Our findings that pretend play is predominantly social and that mothers are heavily involved during the early years is consistent with a growing body of literature (e.g., Dunn 1986; Dunn and Dale 1984; Garvey 1990). In particular, Dunn and Dale (1984) report that during unstructured observations of two year olds, all of whom had older siblings, 33 percent of the episodes of pretend play involved mothers, 16 percent involved older siblings, and 10 percent involved both. This literature provides no support for the view that pretend play develops from a solo to a social activity and suggests that European American middle-class mothers pretend extensively with their children during the early years.

In light of the observational methodology employed in our study, it is necessary to address the effects of the observation procedures on our findings that early pretend play is predominantly social. Because the data were originally collected for a different purpose, awareness that pretend play was the focus of inquiry can be ruled out as a source of distortion. However, mothers were obviously aware of being observed and this may have affected the extent or nature of their participation in pretending. There are two factors that minimize these effects: the care that was taken to establish rapport with the families and the number and length of the observation sessions. Each family was observed for a total of seven sessions, each lasting three to four hours. It seems unlikely that mothers could sustain markedly altered patterns of interactions, especially with very young children, over such extended periods. In addition, we believe that observations of mothers in everyday domestic settings are more likely to yield an accurate picture of their involvement in pretending than are the more typical laboratory-based observations.

In interpreting the finding that mothers were the primary play partners for early pretending, it is important to keep in mind several facts about the social ecology of these families. First, fathers were typically away at work on weekday mornings and thus made only rare appearances on videotape. Although our study cannot speak to the nature of fathers' participation in early pretending, the fact that mothers were the primary caregivers means that they had far more opportunity than fathers to pretend with their children. Previous studies of parent-child interaction suggest that the play styles of fathers and mothers differ, with fathers engaging in more physical, rough-and-tumble play and mothers engaging in more verbal, toy-mediated play (Lamb 1977; Clarke-Stewart 1978; MacDonald and Parke 1986). If mothers and fathers also differ in the ways in which they pretend with their children, future research should address the possibility that children may benefit in different ways from pretending with their fathers, compared with pretending with their mothers.

Second, the family constellations (one to three children per family) and cultural practices (limited exposure to peers during the earliest years, older siblings in school) of this group were such that most of the children had greater access to mothers than peers as play partners, particularly as toddlers. Our finding that mothers were the primary play partners in the second and third years of life thus reflects, in part, social ecological and cultural factors that maximize the availability of mothers as potential interactants. A preliminary analysis suggests that children may also prefer to pretend with mothers, rather than with peers or siblings, at the younger ages. The relative contribution of availability versus preference in accounting for mother as primary play partner needs to be addressed in future studies designed to permit equal access to mothers and peers.

Future research also needs to explore cultural variation in the interpersonal context of early pretending. Children may be socialized into pretending with a variety of partners. For example, reports from rural Indian, rural Guatemalan (Goncu, Rogoff, Mistry 1989), and Yucatec Mayan (Gaskins 1989) communities suggest that although parental involvement in pretend play rarely occurs, toddlers do pretend in the company of older siblings who direct and instruct the younger children. Ethnographic descriptions from central Mexico (Zukow 1989) suggest that older siblings support toddlers' early pretending and that toddlers' play with sibling caregivers is more advanced than their solo pretending. These observations raise the question of how various social ecologies differentially affect the development of pretending.

In the next chapter we will continue to explore the social nature of everyday pretend play. We will examine how pretend play is conducted within our nine European American families, particularly whether mothers participate in a manner supportive of children's emerging abilities to pretend. More specifically, we will consider the construction of conventions of mutuality that coordinate the sharing of pretend play.

5

The Social Conduct Of Everyday Pretending

Twenty-four-month-old Elizabeth is being carried upstairs for a diaper change by her mother. Elizabeth: "My going Sherman Dairy." (Sherman Dairy is the family's favorite dessert restaurant.) Mother: "You're going to Sherman Dairy?" Elizabeth: "Yeah." Mother: "Is Andrew the cook?" (Andrew is a four-year-old friend who is playing with Elizabeth's sister.) Elizabeth: "Yep." (Pause) "*My* cook." Mother, putting Elizabeth on the changing table and beginning to change her, "You're the cook? You can cook with your dishes, right? Do you have some pots and pans?" Elizabeth: "Yep." Mother: "So what are you gonna have at Sherman Dairy? Ice-cream cone?" Elizabeth nods. . . . Mother: "What color ice cream are you gonna have?" Elizabeth: "Pink" Mother: "Pink? Strawberry or cherry?" Elizabeth: "Strawberry." Mother: "Strawberry ice cream! That's one of my favorites." She continues to clean up Elizabeth.

* * *

In this example, Elizabeth initiated a make-believe excursion to which her mother readily responded. The two sustained the pretense through fourteen turns. Elizabeth's mother followed her daughter's lead, while at the same time helping her to elaborate the pretend play. She asked a number of questions that clarified Elizabeth's intentions and suggested thematic elaborations. In this chapter we systematically explore the social conduct of pretend play. We focus on whether mother-child pretend play is mutually engaging, and whether mothers participate in their children's pretend play in a manner likely to facilitate children's acquisition of pretend play.

In the preceding chapter we established that mothers were children's primary play partners during the early years. Of course, demonstrating the existence of maternal participation does not establish that it affects development. Clearly, any effect of mothers' participation on children's pretend play will depend, in part, on the degree to which pretending is constructed as a mutual activity. Isaacs (1937) recognized that mothers participate in their young children's pretending, but discounted their involvement as too passive or too dominating. Mutual involvement would be indicated if both mother and child abided by conventions of mutuality, initiating joint pretending and pretending in response to the other's initiations. Valentine (1937) commented that young children enjoy and seek out adult involvement in their play. Dunn and Wooding (1977) observed that one and a half to two year olds initiated approximately half of the episodes of mother-child pretend play.

Effects of mothers' participation on children's pretend play also will depend upon the manner in which mothers participate throughout the episode. Once a joint pretend episode has been launched, does the mother follow the child's lead (see Winnicott 1971), or does she introduce topics unrelated to the child's pretending? Does the mother simply repeat or reformulate what the child said, or does she add futher information that extends the play? Does the mother prompt the child by means of explicit instructions for transformational actions, or by queries for further appropriate actions? Miller and Garvey found that mothers' involvement in very young children's play included a "great deal of explicit instruction and direction" (1984, p. 116). Although direct instructions may facilitate the entrance of very young children into play, it could impede older children's attempts to elaborate play themes. Miller and Garvey (1984) found that as toddlers became more competent to conduct mother-baby role play independently, mothers' support of the play became less direct. Kavanaugh, Whittington, and Cerbone (1983) found that mothers of two year olds produced more requests for their children to contribute unique material to joint pretend play than mothers of one year olds. Further data are necessary to document the amount and form of information which mothers provide their children throughout the pretend episode, and to document developmental changes in their participation.

Behavioral Codes

The first two analyses considered the opening sequence of the pretend episode. The "initiator" of an episode of social pretend play was the first person to direct pretend play towards the other person. Thus, a child may be engaged in a nonpretend activity such as block building when the mother initiates pretending, or a child may be engaged in solo pretend play when the mother joins in, initiating an episode of social pretend play. For example, thirty-six-month-old Nancy approached her mother and initiated social pretend play, "I'm a cowboy." At twenty-four months, Nancy looked at a toy dog seated in a toy car. Her mother subsequently initiated social pretend play: "Is the doggie going for a ride?" Note that the action produced by the initiator may be verbal (e.g., a transformational statement such as, "I'll be the mommy and you be the baby") or nonverbal (e.g., gesturing as if feeding the other).

A "sustaining response" to an initiation was a pretend action or verbalization relevant to the other's initiation. For example, thirty-six-month-old Nancy announced, "I drive a car," while gesturing as if steering. Her mother responded, "Oh, where are you going?" thereby sustaining the pretense initiated by Nancy. No response to the initiation, explicit refusals to play, or minimal acknowledgments of the social overture (e.g., the mother nods and says "OK" following the child's initial pretend statement) were considered to be nonsustaining.

The next analyses considered mother's verbalizations occurring throughout the episode. "Maternal contingent verbalizations" were defined as verbalizations (complete sentence or independent clause) that were topically related to the child's prior pretend contribution. That is, we were concerned not only with how an episode of social pretending was launched but how mothers participated verbally in the unfolding of the episode. Maternal verbalizations that did not pursue the pretend topic currently in play or which redirected the child in a nonpretend direction were considered noncontingent.

Contingent verbalizations were further coded as either reformulations or elaborations. "Elaborations" extended the child's pretending by adding new material that was thematically related to the preceding play. For example, twenty-four-month-old Nancy pointed and waved a straw at the observer, "Whoosh! I turned you into a frog." Mother replied, "That's quite a magic straw." Elaborations also requested that the child explicate implicit transformations. For example, twenty-four-month-old Elizabeth was making a replica horse pull a pony cart. Mother asked, "Who's pulling the cart?" Elaborations also introduced novel material related to previously established, ongoing pretend themes. For example, when thirty-six-month-old Nancy remarked, "I'm a cowboy," her mother inquired, "Do you want to go get Buster [stick horse] and ride away into the wild blue yonder?" Later, the "cowboy" was pretending to sleep. Mother asked, "Have you been out riding the range? Taking care of the cattle?" Elaborations sometimes replicated portions of the child's transformation, but as long as they also contributed additional information regarding transformations they were considered to be elaborations and not reformulations.

"Reformulations" were contingent verbalizations that did not contribute new content to the ongoing play. Rather, the mother's statement simply clarified or repeated the child's preceding pretend play, but did not contribute new content. For example, a thirty-six-month-old soccer player announced, "We're the Gwendy's!" Her mother reformulated, "Oh, we're the Gwendy's team." Mothers' reformulations frequently "corrected" the child's grammatically incomplete or otherwise illogical, atypical or ambiguous transformation, or requested that the child supply the additional information. For example, thirty-six-month-old Nancy was pretending to put on a puppet show, "Present the wonderful day!" Mother asked, "Presenting the wonderful what?" Later, Nancy gestured as if locking her mother into the pretend bathroom and stated, "You're locked!" Mother replied, "You — Oh, you locked me in the bathroom?" Examples of such reformulations are found in the transcripts of all of the mothers in our study. For example, thirty-six-month-old John was assigning roles. "He [baby brother] could be that red guy." Mother asked, "Spiderman?" John answered, "Yeah." Twenty-four-month-old Michael was driving his mother to the "country." Michael: "A here the country." Mother: "Oh, we're at the country?"

An additional analysis considered whether maternal contingent verbalizations prompted children's pretending. "Maternal prompts" were transformational statements that required a response from the child. Prompts were further coded as either questions or direct instructions. "Direct instructions" prompted the child to produce a pretend action or utterance. For example, a mother instructed her twelve-month-old, "Say, 'Hi Teddy-Tie.'" "Questions" referred to the child's pretend action or utterance. "Yes/no questions" referred to a pretend action or utterance and required a yes/no response. For example, during play thirty-six-month-old Elizabeth's mother queried, "Are you being a baby?" "WH questions" also referred to a pretend action. They required a response explaining where, what, when, why, or how. For example, thirty-six-month-old Kathy wanted to prepare a birthday party for her doll, Diva. Following a pause in the action, her mother inquired of Diva, "Well, who shall we invite to the party? Who's your favorite friend?" And Kathy replied, "Princess Adore."

Intercoder Reliability

Coding for the above analyses was done from written transcripts. Intercoder reliabilities were obtained for portions of the actual transcripts following training. Agreement between two independent raters coding 20 percent to nearly 100 percent of the data at each age ranged from 91 percent to 100 percent across codes. Data used for the reliability checks were randomly chosen from each child at each age level excluding data used for training. One of the raters was naive as to the hypotheses.

Results

Who Initiates Episodes of Mother-Child Pretend Play, and How Responsive Is the Play Partner to these Initiations?

The social conduct of pretend play was assessed first by determining who initiated the episode. There were 43, 105, 100, and 72 episodes of mother-child pretend play observed at twelve,

THE SOCIAL CONDUCT OF EVERYDAY PRETENDING   51

Table 5.1.
Intercoder reliabilities: Percentage agreement

Code	Age in months			
	12	24	36	48
Initiators of episodes[a]	100 (9)	100 (21)	90 (21)	97 (14)
Contingent verbalizations[b]	93 (28)	96 (574)	95 (737)	99 (634)
Elaborations[b]	91 (23)	96 (434)	97 (547)	99 (562)
Prompts[b]	96 (48)	97 (373)	99 (490)	99 (283)
Direct instructions[b]	93 (14)	93 (42)	100 (41)	93 (41)

[a] Based on 20 percent of episodes for each child at each age level.
[b] Based on the total number of relevant responses.

twenty-four, thirty-six, and forty-eight months, respectively. At twelve months, when pretending had barely emerged in the children, children initiated only 1 percent of all episodes of mother-child social pretend play. In contrast, at twenty-four, thirty-six, and forty-eight months, children initiated 41 percent, 58 percent, and 49 percent of the episodes, respectively. (See table 5.2.) (A repeated measures ANOVA on the mean percentage of episodes of mother-child pretending initiated by the child indicated a significant main effect of age, F [3, 23] = 6.04, p < .003.) (Note that a two-way ANOVA was not performed here because the values for mothers and children are not independent. Except for rare instances when a third player initiated the episode, all mother-child pretending was initiated either by the mother or the child.)

Trends for the individual children mirrored group patterns at twelve, thirty-six, and forty-eight months. There was, however, considerable individual variation in the extent to which children initiated pretending at twenty-four months, suggesting variation in children's early competencies. At twenty-four months seven of nine children initiated pretend play with their

Table 5.2.
The mean percentage and SEM of episodes of
mother-child pretend play initiated by the child

	Age in months			
	12	24	36	48
Mean percentage	1	41	58	49
SEM	1	11	4	12
N[a]	43	105	104	70

[a] Total number of episodes observed.

mothers and the range was substantial: one child initiated 0.90 episodes, whereas two children initiated only 0.22 and 0.25 episodes. At thirty-six months there was considerable consistency across the group: all nine children initiated episodes, with a range of only 0.40 to 0.73 episodes. In addition, seven children increased in their rates of initiation from twenty-four months. At forty-eight months, seven children initiated episodes of pretending with their mothers and five of these initiated 0.50 or more of the episodes. In addition, five children increased in their rates of initiation from thirty-six months. Of the eighteen samples encompassing the thirty-six- and forty-eight-month data points, children initiated more episodes in ten samples, mothers initiated more episodes in six samples, and mothers and children initiated equal numbers in two samples. Only one child consistently intitiated fewer episodes than her mother across the entire age range.

Given the finding that mothers and children apparently sought out one another as play partners, we considered the extent to which mothers and children were responsive to one another's initiations. Specifically, what percentage of children's and mothers' initiations of social pretend play did the other respond to with actions or talk supportive of continued pretending? Table 5.3 shows that, with the exception of twelve month olds, both mothers and children generally were responsive to one another's initiations. An Age (24, 36, and 48) by

Player (2) repeated measures ANOVA performed on the mean percentage of sustaining responses to initiations revealed no significant main effects or interactions. Unfortunately, small base figures preclude analysis of trends for the individual mother-child pairs.

Table 5.3.
The mean percentage and SEM of mothers' and children's
sustaining responses to the partner's initiations of
pretend play episodes

	Age in months			
	12	24	36	48
Mothers' sustaining responses to children's initiations				
Mean percentage	100	82	61	52
SEM	0	7	13	16
N^a	1	44	64	38
Children's sustaining responses to mothers' initiations				
Mean percentage	5	48	65	59
SEM	3	10	13	11
N^b	42	59	40	29

[a] Number of episodes initiated by children to their mothers.

To What Extent Are Mothers' Verbalizations During Pretend Play Contingent on the Child's Prior Pretending?

The preceding questions focused on the opening sequence of the pretend episode, i.e. does mother or child launch the pretend episode and how frequently does the other respond to the initiation in a way that sustains the pretense? A related question concerns mothers' verbalizations that occur throughout the episode: how many of these utterances are contingent on prior child pretending, either verbal or nonverbal? There were 170, 710, 861, and 699 mother utterances within episodes of pretend play at twelve, twenty-four, thirty-six, and forty-eight months, respectively. Table 5.4 shows that from the time children were pretending fluently at twenty-four months, the majority of mothers' utterances within episodes of pretend play were contingent on children's preceding pretend actions, verbal or nonverbal. A repeated measures ANOVA on the percentage of mothers' utterances during pretend play that were

Table 5.4.
The mean percentage and SEM of mothers' utterances within pretend play that are contingent responses, and the percentage of contingent responses that are elaborations or reformulations

	Contingent verbalizations	Elaborations	Reformulations
		12 months	
Mean percentage	8	61	39
SEM	6	31	31
N	170[a]	14[b]	
		24 months	
Mean percentage	75	70	30
SEM	8	9	9
N	710	533	
		36 months	
Mean percentage	67	59	41
SEM	12	10	9
N	861	577	
		48 months	
Mean percentage	72	91	9
SEM	12	2	2
N	699	503	

[a] Total number of mother utterances accompanying pretend play.
[b] Total number of contingent responses.

contingent responses revealed a significant main effect of age, F (3, 22) = 7.55, p < 0.001. However, the means presented in table 5.4 show that the increase in mother's contingent responses occurs from twelve to twenty-four months. Not surprisingly, the amount of mothers' contingent responding was low at twelve months, when children produced little pretend play to which mothers could respond contingently.

This overall pattern of contingent mother responding is reflected in the figures for seven of the nine individual mothers: contingent responding accounted for 0.68 or more of mother utterances at every sample for four of the mothers, at two of three samples for three of the mothers, and at one sample for two mothers.

Our next analysis explored the different ways in which mothers' contingent verbalizations were related to the child's preceding pretending. That is, of those mother utterances that were contingent, how many elaborated on the play rather than simply reformulated what the child said? There were 14, 533, 577, and 503 contingent utterances at twelve, twenty-four, thirty-six, and forty-eight months, respectively. Table 5.4 shows that throughout the age range mothers' responses tended to be elaborations. Indeed, elaborations accounted for the majority of individual mothers' contingent responses for all but one mother at twelve and twenty-four months, for all but two mothers at thirty-six months, and for all mothers at forty-eight months. A repeated measures ANOVA on the mean percentage of mother responses that were elaborations revealed no significant main effect of age.

Do Mothers Prompt their Children to Pretend and, if so, How Do Their Prompts Change Developmentally?

Our next question entails further coding of mothers' verbalizations. To what extent do mothers prompt pretending and do the devices they use change developmentally? Table 5.5 shows that mothers prompted their children to pretend throughout the age range. At all ages nearly all mothers produced prompts. A repeated measures analysis of variance on the percentage of mothers' utterances that were prompts revealed no significant main effect of age.

Table 5.5.
The mean percentage and SEM of mothers' total utterances
within pretend play that are prompts, and the percentage of
prompts that are direct instructions and questions

	Prompts	Direct Instructions	Questions
		12 months	
Mean percentage	34	24	76
SEM	8	7	8
N	170[a]	58[b]	
		24 months	
Mean percentage	53	11	89
SEM	3	3	4
N	710	376	
		36 months	
Mean percentage	55	8	92
SEM	9	2	3
N	861	474	
		48 months	
Mean percentage	42	14	86
SEM	4	3	6
N	699	294	

Given the frequency of mothers' prompting, we investigated the types of prompts that were used. Table 5.5 shows that the majority of prompts were questions. Indeed, direct instructions were relatively infrequent. Except for twelve months, when they comprised a mean of 24 percent of mothers' prompts, direct instructions remained below 15 percent of total prompts throughout the age range. Furthermore, a substantial percentage of these questions (ranging from 21 percent at twenty-four months to 44 percent at forty-eight months) were not simple yes/no questions, but required children to respond to the who, what, where, why, or how of their pretending. A repeated measures ANOVA on the percentage of prompts that were direct instructions revealed no significant main effect of age.

Discussion

These analyses of the social conduct of everyday pretending revealed mutually responsive interactions in which both mothers and children initiated and responded to pretending, and mothers elaborated upon and prompted children's pretending. Contrary to Isaacs's (1937) claim, mothers were neither passive nor dominating in their play. This contrasted with other types of mother-child activities such as teaching table manners where mothers were more directive, or watching "Sesame Street" when they tended to be more passive. Similarly, older siblings were somtimes dominating in their play and younger siblings were sometimes passive. The activity of mother-child pretending, however, was characterized by mutual responsiveness. The extent to which norms for mutuality characterize parent-child or sibling pretend play in other cultural groups is unclear as comparable analyses are not available.

Our analyses of initiations of pretend episodes suggest that pretend play with mothers was one-sided only at the earliest age. Virtually any pretending that occurred at twelve months was initiated by the mothers. By twenty-four months, when pretending was fully established in the children, mothers and children showed mutual interest in pretending with one another. At twenty-four months, children initiated approximately half of the episodes of mother-child pretend play, a finding strikingly similar to that reported by Dunn and Wooding (1977) in their study of one and a half to two year olds in home settings. Children continued to initiate roughly half of all episodes of pretend play with mothers at the later ages.

These findings suggest that although pretend play was first introduced by the mothers to twelve month olds, it rapidly became a joint activity constructed according to norms of mutuality. More fine-grained analyses of mother-infant interactions suggest that even ten- to seventeen-month-old children actively negotiate the pretend frame. Beizer (1991) described children's initial attempts at pretending as ambiguous. Parents sometimes responded to such attempts at pretending in a literal manner, eliciting active protests from the children. As children's nonliteral markers became clearer, parents more consistently encouraged infants to engage in more elaborate pretending.

Even at forty-eight months, when a substantial amount of pretending occurred with other children, the focal children continued to initiate pretending with their mothers. Apparently, increasing involvement with other children as play partners did not dampen the children's interest in pretending with their mothers. In addition, both children and mothers were highly responsive to the other's initiations.

Further analyses of mothers' participation in pretend play subsequent to the opening sequence of initiation-response revealed their continuing sensitivity throughout the episode. At twelve months mothers had few opportunities to respond to children's pretend contributions because children pretended so little. Once the children were pretending fluently at twenty-four months, however, the majority of the mothers' verbalizations were contingent on the child's preceding pretend contribution. Moreover, throughout the entire age range, the majority of their contingent verbalizations were thematically related elaborations of the child's pretending. This pattern of contingent, elaborative responding applied not only on average but to the majority of individual mothers. These findings suggest that mothers followed their children's lead in the sense that they inserted their verbalizations into the ongoing play in a way that elaborated on the child's contribution. At the same time, these mothers did a considerable amount of prompting of pretense, and this occurred across the entire age range. In contrast to Miller and Garvey's findings (1984), the majority of prompts were questions rather than direct instructions, and a substantial percentage of these questions required children to elaborate upon the who, what, why, and how of their pretending. These findings point to mothers' sensitivity to the child's moment-by-moment contribution to the interaction while also confirming Kavanaugh, Whittington, and Cerbone's (1983) finding that mothers take responsibility for guiding pretend interactions.

Although the present study established that mothers participate in their children's pretend play in an apparently supportive manner, it remains to be shown that this participation facilitates development. The presence of variation in children's early initiations of pretend play, as well as mothers tendencies to respond contingently to their children, suggests that future research should examine the relation between children's early competencies in pretend play and the extent to which their mothers support their initial attempts to share pretend play.

The present study also specified ways in which mothers support children's early pretend play through prompting and elaborating their children's pretend contributions. It remains to be shown that these particular forms of maternal participation elicit relevant responses from the children. Detailed sequential analyses within pretend episodes are needed to identify the immediate effects of mothers' participation on children's pretend play and of children's responses on mothers' participation. Is it prompts and elaborations or some other aspect of mothers' participation that is responsible for the greater length of episodes with mothers at twenty-four and thirty-six months? To what extent are children's pretend contributions related to mothers' preceding pretend talk? What kinds of mother utterances are children likely to reproduce or respond to with other thematically related verbalizations? In the next chapter we will begin to consider the immediate effects of mothers' participation on the structure and content of pretend play episodes. To what extent do children incorporate their mothers' pretend utterances into their own subsequent pretend play? Are episodes of mother-child pretend play more extended than children's solo pretend play episodes?

6

Immediate Outcomes Of Mothers' Participation in Pretend Play

Example 1: Charlie at thirty months Charlie is sitting with his mother on the floor of his bedroom. He hands his mother a mouse puzzle and she asks, "Are you gonna take it apart?" Charlie answers, "Uhhuh" and then, gazing at the puzzle, speaks in a high-pitched voice: "Bear, I'm gonna take apart you." His mother queries, "Do you think he's a bear or do you think he's a mouse?" and Charlie replies in his normal voice, "I think he's a bear." Mother: "You think he's a bear?" Charlie: "Uhhuh."

While moving the mouse head puzzle piece from side to side, Charlie's mother speaks for the mouse in a high-pitched voice, "Do you fix—, Charlie can you fix me?" and Charlie replies in a high-pitched voice, "OK." Charlie's mother, still speaking for the mouse in a high-pitched voice, responds, "OK." Charlie comments, also in a high-pitched voice, "I would."

Charlie and his mother switch into normal voices to discuss the proper position of the puzzle pieces. Charlie: "Goes up there." Mother: "This goes up there." Charlie: "Goes up there." Mother: "OK."

Charlie's mother resumes talking for the mouse in a high-pitched voice, "Oh little boy are you gonna fix me?" Charlie, replies in a high-pitched voice, "Uhhuh." His mother continues in a high-pitched voice, "Oh good you fixed my head," as Charlie starts to fit the head piece into the puzzle. Unable to get the head piece in place, he picks up a foot piece and announces, "I fix you feet," using normal voice. His mother answers in a high-pitched voice, "You fixed my feet. Good. That's hard work."

Charlie and his mother continue to work on and discuss the puzzle for several more minutes.

Example 2: Charlie at thirty-six months Charlie and his mother are sitting on the floor in Charlie's bedroom. Charlie is pushing a toy train. In the train are Fisher-Price people. Sitting on top of the train are a rabbit and another animal. The rabbit has fallen off the train. Charlie, speaking for the rabbit, exclaims in a high-pitched voice, "Ohhhh. I'm off the train! Help me! I'm off the train! I'm off the train! I'm off the train! I'm off the train!" Charlie's high-pitched voice now takes on a whine: "Come on. Come on," and he begins to play-cry, "Waah! Waah!" His mother asks in a normal voice, "Is he cryin'?" Charlie says, "No" in a deep-pitched, stern voice as he repeatedly hits the rabbit with a Fisher-Price person. His mother continues her inquiry,

"Why did he get a spanking?" Charlie, speaking in a normal voice, "Because he couldn't get on the train because he had a balloon." Charlie and his mother continue to discuss why the rabbit cannot board the train with a balloon. Then, Charlie turns back towards the train and, continuing to use a normal voice, directs his mother, "You get the keeper" (the zookeeper figure). She replies for the zookeeper in a high-pitched voice, "Here I come," while making noises and "walking" the zookeeper towards Charlie. Switching into a normal voice, she says, "There he is." Then speaking as the conductor, Charlie addresses the Fisher-Price people on the train in a deep-pitched, stern voice, "You want to get out?" The play continues for several minutes.

* * *

In these examples Charlie's mother consistently used a high-pitched voice when animating objects. At thirty months, Charlie also adopted this communicative device, although he employed it inconsistently and not entirely appropriately. In contrast to his mother who used a high-pitched voice when speaking *for* the mouse, Charlie used this device when speaking *to* the mouse. He seemed to understand that pitch is a marker in pretend play, but he had not yet grasped how it functions to mark contrasting roles. By thirty-six months, however, Charlie used pitch in a manner that was similar to his mother's usage: he not only employed high-pitched voice accurately and consistently in animating the rabbit but he added a contrasting deep-pitched voice to mark his own role, apparently that of conductor. Both of these "marked" voices were further differentiated from his normal voice which was reserved for "out-of-role" instructions to his mother. We thus see the emergence of Charlie's ability to mark roles within the context of recurring pretend interactions in which his mother had earlier used pitch contrastively. This example suggests an important question that has arisen as researchers have begun to explore the social dimensions of pretend play: What role do caregivers play in the emergence and early development of pretending?

Immediate Outcomes of Mothers' Participation in Pretending

In this chapter we consider whether mothers' participation in their children's pretending affects the structure and content of the pretend episode. Mothers' participation in their children's early pretend play, particularly their tendencies to respond to and prompt pretending, raise the issue of whether such practices help to sustain children's play. There is some evidence that toddlers' pretend play with mothers is more sustained than their solo pretending (Dunn and Wooding 1977; Slade 1987), suggesting that maternal participation affects the structure of the pretend episode. The analysis presented in this chapter offers the opportunity to verify this finding and to determine whether this relation changes developmentally. Comparing the length of children's pretend episodes involving other children and mothers will illuminate the relative advantage of pretending with mothers versus other children.

A second type of evidence relevant to assessing the immediate outcomes of mothers' participation concerns the extent to which children actually incorporate caregivers' verbal transformations into their own subsequent pretending within or across episodes. The degree to which children replicate or reproduce their mothers' utterances provides a conservative estimate of the content children take from their mother's contribution to the play. Empirical studies have yet to examine the extent to which children directly incorporate caregiver models of pretend play into their own subsequent play.

Behavioral Codes

The first analysis concerned the relative length of pretend episodes that did or did not involve a partner. Episodes with mother, solo episodes, and episodes with other children were compared. We considered as solo only those episodes in which no other person was involved (e.g., solo segments of episodes in which mothers initiated and then withdrew from the pretending were not considered). Similarly, episodes of mother-child play and play with other children involved only mother or other children and not both.

The second analysis focused on "child reproductions" which were defined as:

1. Exact imitations of the mother's transformational statement (e.g., when twelve-month-old Nancy's mother implicitly animated a stuffed bear by greeting it, "Hi," Nancy likewise greeted the bear, "Hi.").

2. Reproductions of the signifier and the signified of mother's pretend utterance with words omitted or added (e.g., twenty-four-month-old Elizabeth's mother asked, "Are you the chef?" and Elizabeth responded, "My chef." Elizabeth was credited with a reproduction because both the person and the role transformation were encoded even though "my" did not appear in the mother's utterance and "the" was omitted from the child's utterance).

3. A reproduction in which the signifier was not verbally explicated but could be inferred from the nonverbal context (e.g., twenty-four-month-old Kathy's mother inquired, "Are you Cinderella?" Later, Kathy, who was dancing while wearing a fancy cape, stated, "Cinderella.").

Included in this definition were utterances that repeated immediately preceding maternal utterances and those that repeated maternal utterances that occurred earlier in the episode or even in a prior pretend episode during the observation session. However, 0.81 of all child reproductions repeated mother utterances that occurred within the same episode.

Intercoder Reliability

Coding for the above analyses was done from written transcripts. Intercoder reliabilities were obtained for portions of the actual transcripts following training. Agreement between two independent raters coding 100 percent of the data at each age was 90 percent, 89 percent, 75 percent and 83 percent at twelve, twenty-four, thirty-six and forty-eight months, respectively. Data used for the reliability checks were randomly chosen from each child at each age level excluding data used for training. One of the raters was naive as to the hypotheses.

Results

Immediate Outcomes of Mother Participation at the Local Discourse Level

Are Episodes of Pretend Play Involving Mothers More Sustained than Children's Solo Pretend Play?

At twenty-four months, the mean length of children's episodes of pretend play with their mothers was twice as sustained as their solo pretend play (see table 6.1), and this pattern of longer episodes with mothers held for all six individual children who engaged in both solo and mother-child pretending. Similarly, at thirty-six months, the mean length of children's episodes of pretend play with their mothers was twice as sustained as their solo pretend play, and this pattern of longer episodes with mothers held for four of the five children engaging in both solo and mother-child pretend play. (Note, however, that at thirty-six months there was one outlier, Charlie, who was not included in this analysis. Charlie produced only one extremely long solo episode lasting twenty-one minutes. The next longest solo episode produced by any child at thirty-six months was only 3.5 minutes long.) At forty-eight months, the pattern that applied at twenty-four and thirty-six months is reversed, with episodes of solo pretending being twice as sustained as pretending with mothers. This pattern of more sustained solo pretending held for three of the five children who engaged in both solo and mother-child pretending.

This developmental pattern is illuminated by preliminary data available on the duration of peer play at thirty-six and forty-eight months. At thirty-six months, three children pretended with peers and the mean length of mother-child pretend play (114 seconds æ 34) was more sustained than peer play (77 seconds ± 22), and peer play was roughly equivalent in length to solo pretending. At forty-eight months, the mean episode length of pretend play with peers (234 seconds ± 68) was about four times longer than mother-child pretend play (51 seconds ± 29) and about twice as long as solo pretending (124 seconds ± 97). These findings suggest that through thirty-

Table 6.1.
The mean length and SEM in seconds of children's episodes
of solo pretend play and pretend play with mother

	Solo		Mother
		24 months	
Mean	24		51
SEM	8		8
Total episodes	15		75
Total children	6		9
		36 months	
Mean	48[a]		111
SEM	16		34
Total episodes	23		73
Total children	6		8
		48 months	
Mean	124		51
SEM	97		29
Total episodes	14		45
Total children	6		8

six months, mother-child pretend play was more sustained than solo pretending. At forty-eight months, this pattern was reversed but pretend play with peers was more sustained than either mother-child or solo pretending.

How Frequently Do Children Verbally Reproduce their Mothers' Pretend Talk?

Our final question concerns the percentage of children's utterances accompanying mother-child pretend play that replicate aspects of the mother's preceding pretend talk. Table 6.2 shows that a substantial amount of children's talk accompanying pretend play replicated mothers' transformational talk at twelve and twenty-four months, with lower levels occurring at thirty-six and forty-eight months. While only four children produced utterances during mother-child pretend play at twelve months, most of these utterances were reproductions. By twenty-four months, all children produced reproductions during mother-child pretend play, and a mean percentage of thirty were reproductions. For six individual children, reproductions comprised twenty-five or more of children's utterances accompanying mother-child pretend play. By thirty-six months, the mean percentage of reproductions was only five, and at forty-eight months, the mean percentage of reproductions was two. A repeated measures ANOVA on the mean percentage of children's reproductions accompanying mother-child pretend play revealed a main effect of age, F (3, 19) = 15.81, $p < 0.0001$.

Table 6.2.
The mean percentage of children's total utterances accompanying mother-child pretend play that reproduce their mothers' preceding pretend talk

	Age in months			
	12	24	36	48
Mean percentage	75	30	5	2
SEM	25	6	1	1
N[a]	24	573	984	1175

[a] Total number of children's utterances of pretend play.

Discussion

This chapter considered the effects of mothers' participation on pretending. Previous research has shown that toddlers' pretend play with caregivers is more sustained (Dunn and Wooding 1977; Slade 1987), complex (Fiese 1987; Slade 1987), and diverse (O'Connell and Bretherton 1984) than solo pretending, suggesting that mothers' participation has an effect on the structure of early pretend episodes. Our findings are consistent for the twenty-four- and thirty-six-month data: episodes of pretend play were at least twice as long when the children pretended with their mothers as when they pretended on their own. However, a different picture emerged at forty-eight months when solo pretending was twice as long as pretend episodes with the mother. In addition, at forty-eight months episodes involving peers as play partners were twice as long as solo episodes. These findings suggest that pretending with a partner yields longer episodes at all ages, but that at forty-eight months it is peers rather than mothers who confer this advantage.

The present analyses also assessed the extent to which children actually incorporate caregiver models of pretend play into their own pretending. A substantial percentage of children's utterances accompanying their early pretending (at twelve and twenty-four months) reproduced their mothers' pretend talk. By thirty-six and forty-eight months, however, reproductions accounted for a very small percentage of children's talk accompanying pretend play. These findings raise the possibility that mothers' participation has its greatest impact on children's entrance into pretend play. It should also be noted that reproductions provide an incomplete assessment of the extent to which children—especially older, more verbally sophisticated children—build upon their mothers' pretend contributions. For example, they may respond in a manner that is topically relevant without replicating the mother's verbalization. Further analyses are needed to examine more comprehensively the extent to which the child's pretend contribution relates to the mother's prior verbalization.

Future research also should investigate longer-term effects of mother-child pretend play. In particular, do the lessons learned during mother-toddler play influence subsequent play with peers? The first step in addressing this question is to determine whether or not there is a relationship between individual variation in characteristics of mother-toddler pretending and subsequent peer play. Although our investigations of the social nature of pretending point to considerable consistency within this homogeneous sample of mothers, there were some striking individual differences and these differences may account, in part, for differences observed in the children. For example, although every mother pretended with her child, the extent of mother participation varied greatly from 0.1 to 1.00 minute per hour at twelve months, 1.00 to 4.00 minutes per hour at twenty-four months, 0.01 to 10.00 minutes per hour at thirty-six months and 0 to 10 minutes per hour at forty-eight months. Correspondingly, of the six children for whom mother data at twelve months and peer data at forty-eight months are available, the children whose mothers ranked first and second in frequency of pretending at twelve months ranked first and second, respectively, in frequency of peer pretend play at forty-eight months. In addition, there were some obvious qualitative differences in the extent to which mothers seemed to enjoy pretending, and the extent to which they contributed fairly stereotyped or highly imaginative themes. The children of our most enthusiastic and imaginative mothers also were highly skilled pretenders.

If early mother-child pretend play is associated with children's emerging abilities to pretend with peers, then the next step is to identify mediating variables. Language is likely to provide one such link (Dunn 1986; Garvey 1990; Sachs 1980). Communicating with a partner about pretend transformations is necessary for social pretending, and recent research by Garvey and Kramer (1989) shows that the language of pretend play is a specialized use of language. Communicative devices encountered initially in pretend play with mother may carry over into pretend play with peers (Miller and Garvey 1984). Establishing a causal relationship, however, is difficult. As Dunn (1986) has pointed out, if aspects of child behavior are found to be related to mothers' involvement in pretend play, we cannot infer that there is a causal link between mothers' participation in pretending and child outcomes. Mothers who pretend a great deal with their children also may use language differently in nonpretend contexts and this may have an effect on the child's language development.

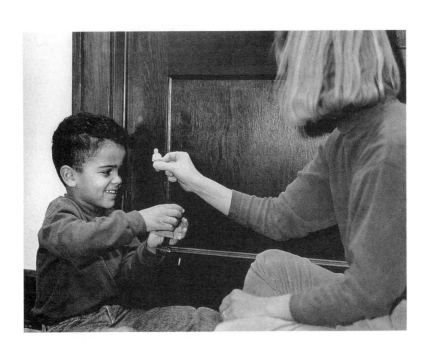

7

The Social Functions of Everyday Pretending

During lunchtime three-year-old John and his mother engage in an extended conflict. John throws his napkin on the floor. His mother demands that he pick it up, and, eventually, he complies. He is then excused from the table. He runs through the living room "shooting" his "ray gun" (a plastic trumpet). He turns, smiling, "I see a bad guy. . . . You saw I got him? You saw arrow in the head? . . . I popped him right in the leg. . . ." Then, addressing the imaginary bad guy, "Come on big bad guy! Pick them up right now!" John runs and jumps across the room making large arm gestures as if heaving the screaming bad guy towards the open cabinet. "I put him right in . . ." Then, shouting to the bad guy while slamming the cabinet doors, "Never come back out!. . ." John hums as he walks over to a child-sized picnic table and crawls under announcing, "I'm going in my little house."

* * *

This pretend episode, in which John attacks a sloppy "bad guy" and commands him to "pick them up right now!," is occasioned by an extended conflict in which John's mother prevails in her demand that John pick up his napkin. As we watched pretend play unfold we were struck by its intimate connection to the ongoing social scene and to issues of obvious personal significance to the players. We came to appreciate the many ways in which pretending evolved out of and alluded to ordinary family interactions, with their inevitable variety and depth of emotion. Children and their mothers pretended for the sheer fun of it. But they also used pretend play to express and regulate feelings, support an argument, enliven daily routines, teach, and influence the other's behavior. We also noticed patterns of individual variation in the ways in which pretend play functioned for mothers and children. In this chapter we present some qualitative descriptions of particular mother-child dyads which raise important questions for future studies of the social functions of everyday pretending.

Communicating Feelings

The intense, expressive, and uninhibited pretend play of Joe and his mother provides a good illustration of how some mothers and children use pretending to communicate about emotionally significant topics and to regulate their feelings. Considering the extent to which mother's participate in children's pretending, the possibility that pretend play is a context for the socialization of affect should be explored (see Dunn, 1986).

Joe lived in a large apartment in Chicago with his parents and brother Alex, who was about two years younger. Joe enjoyed playing with other children at home and at a babysitter's house, but his most elaborate and expressive play occurred with his mother. They rode in boats (an unfilled wading pool), drove boats (small weights) through a river (a mixture of cornstarch and water), cooked dinner, fed the stuffed monkey lunch, put out fires, and endured the painful punches of Spiderman. For Joe, pretending with his mother could be a vehicle for the expression of intense feelings which, in ordinary life, generated many conflicts. In particular, Joe and his mother had numerous arguments over Joe's rough treatment of his baby brother.

At forty-eight months, Joe's pretend play revealed complex feelings about his baby brother. In three episodes of pretend play initiated by Joe and encompassing over thirteen minutes of observation, he assumed the role of a very naughty baby and his mother scolded him with exaggerated severity while expressing concern for the endangered baby. For example, Joe and Alex had climbed on top of a wardrobe in the basement. Joe, smiling, reached up and touched a pipe hanging from the ceiling, "Hot!" Mother: "Don't touch it. You'll get burned. Hot! Joe hot!" Joe continued to touch the pipe on the ceiling, smiling. Mother, with exaggerated severity, as she attempted to restrain Joe's arm while he managed to touch the pipe several more times: "Joe you're gonna get burned! No Joe! No! It's hot! No, hot! Don't touch something hot. You'll get burned!" Joe made baby vocalizations. Mother pulled Joe down as he screamed like a baby and managed to touch the pipe several more times:"No, baby! No! I'll take you away from there, baby. No, baby, you can't touch something hot! No, baby that's dangerous. No! I'm gonna put you down, baby! Come on, baby. Come on. Come on, baby. That's dangerous." As soon as Joe's mother put him down he climbed back up on the wardrobe and touched the pipe: "I'm baby. I'm gonna touch something hot!" His mother warned while holding his hand: "Nope, nope, nope! No, Baby, no! It'll hurt your hand. I'm gonna slap you if you do that again." Joe smiled broadly and they continued in this vein for five more minutes.

Later in the observation, as Joe and his mother made play dough, he introduced another pretend theme that reveals complex negative feelings about his baby brother. Before the play dough had been cooked, Joe spooned the runny, gooey mixture over his arm. Mother: "What's that?" Joe, with markedly dampened affect: "It's Alex doo-dooing all over me." Mother: "Alex's doo-dooing all over you? Why's he doing that?" Joe: "Because he can't go to the toilet fast." Mother: "Ohh! Maybe we better keep a diaper on him." Joe: "No —" Mother: "You like it when he does that?" Joe, continued to spoon the mixture over his arm, "No. He's already doing it. Why is Alex doing it?" Mother: "You just told me. Because he couldn't get to the bathroom on time." Joe: "No, but why is he doo-dooing all over me?" Mother: "Well, I don't know. Why do you think he's doing it?" Joe: "Because. He want to. He think it funny." Mother: "Is it funny? What do you think of it?" Joe continued to pour the mixture over his arm "He's doing it all over my arm too. Alex's bad. Alex's doing it all over my arm. I don't like that." Several minutes later Joe initiated a second episode in which he discussed why his baby brother "doo-doos" on him.

Arguing

Although pretending and arguing might appear to be mutually exclusive activites, pretend play sometimes evolves out of serious conflicts, as in the opening example to this chapter, raising questions about the extent to which pretending may be used to resolve or diffuse conflict. Indeed, Garvey and Shantz (1992) have observed the incorporation of pretend play into naturally occurring conflict. They observed children acting "as if" they were having a conflict as well as opposing one another without abandoning the pretend frame. The elaborate and complex play of Nancy and her mother provide numerous examples of both subtypes of conflict within pretend play.

Nancy lived with her parents and brother David, approximately three years older. While she had frequent contact with other children, Nancy was fortunate to be guided into pretending by a mother who was highly imaginative and clearly relished pretend play. At the age of thirty months, Nancy pretended to argue with her mother. In one episode she instructed her mother while jumping on the couch, "Say, 'Don't jump on the couch.' You say some, you say, 'Don't jump on the couch!'" Her mother answered in an appropriately stern and emphatic voice, "Nancy, don't jump on the couch!" Nancy smiled and continued to jump, "No!" The pretend conflict continued in this vein for several more turns.

At the age of thirty-six months, Nancy and her mother incorporated real conflicts into their play without abandoning the pretend frame. For example, Nancy's mother tried to convince her to give up her pacifier (an effort which Nancy resisted), occasioning a number of conflicts. In one episode of pretending, Nancy and her mother were animating two mittens with faces sewn onto the hands, when Nancy announced, "I want a pacifier." Then she addressed the request to her mother's mitten, "I want a pacifier." Mother: "Little girl, you just have a red dot on your face for a mouth. I don't think you can fit a pacifier in your mouth." Nancy examined the mitten's mouth, "I could fit a pacifier in my mouth." Mother replied, "Oh, I guess so. But then Wendy wouldn't be able to understand what you're talking about." Nancy smiled at Wendy, "Nooo" and continued to examine the mitten. The play continued for several minutes when Nancy announced, "I want two pacifiers." Her mother answered in a high voice, addressing Nancy's mitten, "You may not have two pacifiers." The conflict continued for several more minutes until the issue was simply dropped.

Enlivening Daily Routines

Another function of pretend play is to enliven daily routines and chores. The highly imaginative play of Molly and her mother provide numerous examples of the use of pretending to relieve boredom. Like Nancy, Molly was fortunate to be ushered into pretending by a skillful and highly receptive mother. As a preschool child she also had extensive access to other children including her sister Rachael, approximately three years older. Through the age of two, however, Molly's primary pretend play partner was her mother, who managed to engage with Molly in pretending while preparing meals, running errands, and cleaning house.

In this next example, twenty-four-month-old Molly was sitting on the floor of her bedroom folding laundry with her mother. Molly folded a pair of socks together: "Mommy, look what I made. I made us something to eat." She held the socks up to her mouth and gestured as if eating an ice-cream cone. Later, her mother picked up on the pretend theme and while sorting through the socks noted, ". . . that's your. . . ice-cream sock."

Later in the day, Molly and her mother were in the car, driving to pick up Molly's older sister at preschool. Molly, smiling, said, "A snake." Mother replied, "A snake?" Molly: "Uhhuh." Mother: "Where is there a snake?" Molly points to the window. Mother: "Out the window?" Molly: "Uhhuh. Out my window." Mother: "Out your window is a snake! Is it a little snake or a big snake?" Molly: "A big snake. A snake gone away." Mother: "It's gone away?" Molly: "Yeah." Mother: "Bye-bye snake." Molly: "It's out my window. It's out my window again." Mother: "It's out your window again?" Molly: "Umhm." Mother: "Is it peeking at you? Is it going, 'Sss.'?" Molly: "I want my blankie with my snakes. My snakes." Mother: "Yes. Your blanket will take care of any snake."

Teaching

Throughout this book we have considered how caregivers socialize children into pretend play. However, pretend play may also serve as a vehicle for teaching other lessons. For example, Michael's mother deliberately used pretend play when teaching him to use the toilet. Michael, who was initially quite reluctant, became an eager and successful learner when put in charge of instructing his hesitant baby bear. Nancy's mother enacted an upcoming trip to the shoe store one morning while dressing Nancy, measuring her foot and inquiring about her preferences for shoes.

Even when pretend play is not used as a deliberate teaching device, however, pretending with a caregiver exposes children to a great deal of information concerning social roles, scripts, and conventions. For example, Elizabeth's mother assisted her, along with her older sister and several friends, in setting up and enacting an elaborate restaurant scenario complete with homemade menus, customers, and credit cards.

In another complex episode on a similar theme, thirty-month-old Nancy and her mother created an ice-cream restaurant, with Nancy in the role of waitress. Her mother, in the role of customer, artfully elaborated and guided the portrayal, even introducing monetary compensation for the ice cream. For her part, Nancy demonstrated great sensitivity to the direction offered by her mother, including her corrections of inaccuracies in Nancy's portrayal.

Nancy: "We wanna make a, we wanna make a house. We wanna make a ice-cream store." Nancy began pushing sofa cushions. Her mother responded, "OK," and began moving pillows to form an enclosure. Nancy: "We want ice-cream store," as she climbed into the "store." Her mother asked, "Should it have a roof on it?" while making a pillow roof. Nancy had begun to bounce in the ice-cream store and didn't respond.

Mother said, "OK. Should I be the customer?" Nancy responded, loudly, "What do you like?" Mother: "I like, ah, pralines and cream. Do you have pralines and cream?" Nancy: "Ahh," and went behind the pillow wall, peered at the back of the pillow and then emerged from behind the pillow. "Just pralines and cream. Not pralines." Her mother: "Oh, you just have cream, you don't have pralines and cream?" Nancy: "No." Mother: "Well do you have peppermint-spangled banana-bubblegum?" Nancy said, "Ahh," and repeated her ear-

lier actions behind the pillow wall. "I didn't have that."
Mother: "Oh, you don't?" Nancy: "No." Mother: "OK. Do you
have tutti-frutti, nutty-whaty, tootsie-wootsie ice cream?"
Nancy said, "Ahh," and repeated her earlier actions behind the
pillow wall. "I don't have ice-cream tootsie-wootsie ice cream."
Mother, with mock exasperation, "Well, Madam, what kind of
ice cream do you have?" Nancy, also exasperated, "OK. If I
have that I will give it to you." Mother: "OK." Nancy went
behind the pillow and announced, "I have that," and came out
from behind the pillow. "I have, I have, I have two ice creams
for you," as she made grabbing gestures towards the pillow
wall, holding her fists clenched. Mother: "You have coconut
and banana?" Nancy: "I have, I have two ice creams for you.
And I have a banana for you." Mother: "OK. Great." Mother
held out her fist, and Nancy gestured twice as if giving, un-
clenching her fists.

Mother: "OK. How much money do I owe you?" Nancy:
"Fifty dollars." Nancy held hand open and out. Mother, with
mock surprise, "Fifty dollars! This is the most expensive ice
cream I've ever heard of! Wouldn't fifty cents be OK?" Nancy:
"I have a regtister (sic)." Mother: "You have a cash register?"
Nancy: "Yeah." Mother: "Could I give you fifty cents for each
ice-cream cone?" Nancy: "Yes." Nancy and her mother gesture
as if giving and receiving. Mother: "OK, fine. Thank you very
much. You're so much more reasonable than I first imagined."
Nancy went behind the pillows and gestured as if pushing the
buttons of a cash register. She came out from behind pillows
and the play continued for another nine and one-half minutes.

Managing Others

Pretend play is usually defined as intrinsically motivated, directed to no goal external to the play itself (see Rubin, Fein, and
Vandenberg 1983). Pretend play is enjoyable, at least in part,
because it serves a number of intrapsychic functions, such as
allowing unrealizable desires to be realized in imagination
(Vygotsky 1978) or assimilating the real world to the ego
(Piaget 1962). In several of the examples discussed above, how-

ever, pretend play appears to function strategically in pursuit of interactional goals, such as the resolution of disputes. The following examples from the observations of Molly illustrate how pretend play was used to achieve other social goals.

Twenty-four-month-old Molly was hesitating at the head of the slide. Molly: "Mom, *help* me." Mom: "I'm right here. . . . Climb down . . ." Molly: "I can't." Mom: "Sure you can. You do it all the time." Molly: "No. I want down. . . . Fall down." Mom: "You won't fall down." (Pause) Molly: "A shark come. . . . There's a shark come. . . . There's a shark in the sand." (They began to pretend about the shark in the sand as Molly's mother helped her down.)

Thirty-month-old Molly was sitting with her mother and sister folding socks. Molly made repeated, unsuccessful bids for her sister's fancy socks with lacy decals. Finally she announced, "I *need* them for the birthday party." The sisters and their mother then planned a pretend birthday party while Molly sat happily with the socks in her lap.

Forty-eight-month-old Molly was playing with her toys while her mother sat nearby comforting her screaming infant. Molly: "Mommy, I picked up *all* the doll dresses." The baby continued to cry and Molly's mother did not respond. Molly stood watching her mother and brother. Then, she held out a toy pan with a round plastic stacking block inside of it, "Mommy, would you like a bagel?" Her mother made gestures as if chewing while the baby continued to cry, "Delicious bagel . . ."

In these examples, Molly made repeated attempts to gain her mother's help or attention, or to retain possession of a coveted object. These goals are reached following the strategic initiation of pretend play, suggesting that at least some of the time, pretend play can be a social tool, an *instrumental* strategy for managing the behavior of others.

Having Fun

Of course, much of the time pretend play is engaged in purely for fun. For example, Justin and his mother and younger sister regularly visited a playground near their home, where Justin's mother willingly joined in his pretending, sometimes assuming the role of monster. Mother, growling as she ran after Justin, said, "Here comes the monster!" Justin laughed and ran. His mother continued: "Ahhhhhhh! Now the monster's got you!" Justin laughed as his mother kissed him.

Elizabeth, at the age of forty-eight months, shared her most elaborate fantasies with her sister Rachel, who was about three years older. The sisters particularly relished being silly as they talked in a baby-talk lingo for their two baby dolls. In this example, Rachel began by tickling the feet of Elizabeth's baby doll, "Tickle, tickle." Elizabeth responded for the baby in a high-pitched voice, "Tickle me more." Rachel: "Tickle, tickle" and then ran out the door. Elizabeth followed after her. Holding up her baby doll she spoke for it, demanding, "Tickle! Want tickle! Want tickle." Elizabeth followed Rachel into her bedroom where Rachel got her own baby doll and they returned to Elizabeth's room. . . . Rachel sat on Elizabeth's bed smiling, bouncing the baby doll on her lap and clapping the doll's hands together. Elizabeth noticed a pine cone on the bed and spoke for her baby, demanding, "Pie-coe! Want pie-coe!" Rachel spoke in a very grown-up mother voice and remarked to Elizabeth's doll: "Here's a little pine cone just like you." . . . . . Rachel sang as her baby doll, dancing the doll from side to side, "Ah-ah-ah-ah-ah." . . . Rachel tickled Elizabeth's doll: "Ha, ha, ha, ha, ha, ha, ha," and made her doll dance on her lap. The play continued in this vein for another seven minutes.

Summary

These descriptions suggest that pretend play arises out of ongoing domestic activities and emotional concerns and that it can be used strategically by mother and child to influence one another. Further research should examine these functions in greater depth and detail, including emotion socialization and regulation within the context of pretend play (Dunn 1986), the relationship between pretend play and conflict, the coordination of pretend and nonpretend activities, and the use of pretend play to achieve interpersonal goals.

8

The Physical Ecology of Everyday Pretending

It is the second hour of continuous observation. Forty-eight-month-old Michael is playing in the family playroom while his mother helps his brother and sister get dressed nearby. He is sitting in front of a large, Victorian-style doll house animating various toy action figures. He makes the "Ghostbuster" action figure climb onto the roof of the doll house: "Hey! Ghostbusters alive!" Michael then enacts a conversation between the two heroes, alternately animating Ghostbuster and Captain America. Captain America: "Hey man, how did you get up to the rooftop?" Ghostbuster: "Ah — I don't know how I did that." Captain America: "And where's the ghosts you talked about?" Ghostbuster: "Up there." Captain America: "Wooooooo! Ghosts. Oh." Michael makes explosion sound effects, "POW! POW!" Captain America: "There's some ghosts." (Michael makes more explosions.) Captain America and the Ghostbuster count the ghosts between explosions.

The conversation continues. Ghostbuster: ". . . It's a real haunted house! Don't you think it's a great plan to do this?" (Michael removes the doll house roof.) Captain America: "No, I don't think. I'm just gonna see if I'm not — we're in trouble! OK. . . . but where are you going?" Ghostbuster: "We're going on the roof." Michael walks around to the other side of the house. Ghostbuster: "Well it's pretty haunted up there." Captain America: "It's not pretty haunted. It's real haunted. Where are the ghosts?" Ghostbuster: "I think the ghosts are on the other side of the roof." Captain America: "Maybe they are over on the other side of the roof." Ghost: "Wooooooo!" Michael walks the figures to the other side of the roof, screaming as Captain America falls from the roof. Then he goes to the other side of the house and takes a handful of furniture from downstairs and puts it upstairs. Ghostbuster: "Bam!! There's some ghost. Ah-ah-ah bssh!" Michael makes Ghostbuster fall and produces more sound effects as he drops furniture from the top floor. Ghostbuster: "That's three ghosts." Michael makes more sound effects as he drops out more furniture. "That's three ghosts you see. All right? All right? That's five ghosts. I'm gonna shoot you guys. Get the furniture back up. OK. Here you go babies." Michael makes more sound effects as he drops furniture from the roof to the floor. The pretending continues in this vein for another twenty-four minutes with occasional comments to and from Michael's mother.

* * *

In chapters 4 through 7 we discovered that everyday pretending is social in a variety of ways: it is typically conducted with a partner, it is mutually sustained by the interactants, and it serves a variety of interpersonal functions. This episode of solo pretending illustrates further social dimensions of pretending at the level of physical ecology. First, Michael pretended with specialized objects, such as Superhero action figures, provided by his parents. This suggests an indirect route by which adults influence the everyday practice of pretending, namely as providers of suggestive play props. These objects also reflect parental beliefs about the age and gender appropriateness of toys. Second, Michael enacts this episode in a communal location, a playroom, with other family members comfortably present and available for recruitment into the pretend game. Third, the very existence of a playroom—a room set aside for recreation and the storage of toys—reflects adult assumptions about the value of play. This is not to say that Michael exercised no selectivity in relation to these cultural practices. Indeed, at Christmas time he and his brother asked for action figures, and their younger sister asked for baby dolls. When Michael incorporated his sister's doll house into his play, he did so in a manner that was exciting and meaningful to him—not in the manner envisioned by the provider of this elaborate gift.

Many teachers and researchers view the physical context as important in shaping young children's play, with important practical and methodological implications. When setting up a preschool or kindergarten classroom, or when planning a laboratory study of play, considerable time and thought is devoted to the selection and arrangement of objects. Nevertheless, very little systematic research describes the physical ecology of children's spontaneous play. Insights concerning how to bridge the gap between the practices and ideologies of the home and school, as well as how to elicit the most sophisticated pretending from young children, may be gained from systematic observations of children's preferences for toys and locations, and consideration of how long one must be present to observe children's most frequent and extended pretending. For example, although Michael was obviously capable of creating purely imaginary characters (e.g. ghosts), or transforming objects to fit into his imaginary world, most of his pretend play involved the use of replica objects (e.g. the doll house, Ghostbusters, and Captain America). Also, the fact that Michael's elaborate pretend episode occurred only after the observation session was well underway may reflect his sensitivity to the presence of the observer.

In this chapter we present the analyses and discussion pertaining to the physical ecology of naturally occurring pretend play. We will consider the objects that children use when pretending, the places in which they pretend, and the times during the observation session when their pretend play is most frequent and sustained.

Object Use in Play

There is considerable agreement that objects do affect children's pretend play (e.g., Newson and Newson 1979; Pulaski 1973; Singer 1973; Vygotsky 1978). When describing a child's play with a stick horse Vygotsky (1978) argued that ". . . in order to imagine a horse, he needs to define his action by means of using 'the-horse-in-the-stick' as a pivot." Newson and Newson (1979), who describe toys as the "pegs on which to hang our play," suggest that ". . . because the human imagination is so extensive and complex. . . children seem to look for solid and tangible reference points, as it were, from which to range more freely. Just as language makes subtle and complicated thought possible, perhaps toys do the same for play" (p. 12). Montessori (1973), who argued that pretend play does not facilitate development, designed her educational materials to discourage pretending.

Contemporary quasi-experimental research supports theoretical accounts of the importance of objects in pretend play, and documents developmental changes in the ways in which objects are used (e.g., Fein and Apfel 1979; Garvey 1990; Pulaski 1973; Rocissano 1982; Watson and Fischer 1977). The physical characteristics of objects shape the pretense of very young toddlers which is enhanced by the presence of realistic toys. Between nineteen and twenty-four months, children develop the ability to substitute one object for another, e.g., a block for a cup. By preschool age, the physical characteristics of the objects themselves can be subordinated to the child's preexisting plan for pretend play. Indeed, by preschool age, less realistic objects are associated with an increased diversity of play themes. Garvey (1990) suggests that less realistic objects afford more scope for inventiveness, allowing the preschool-aged child to transform them to fit the play. McLoyd (1983), however, found that during laboratory play sessions preschool children pretended more frequently when given access to replica toys such as tea sets, dolls, and trucks in contrast to objects such as pipe cleaners, boxes, and blocks. This finding raises the possibility that while preschool children may be capable of pretending with a range of objects, they prefer to pretend with replica toys. There are, however, no systematic descriptions of the extent to which children spontaneously use replicas and other types of toys in their pretending at home, and whether these choices change developmentally.

Although objects are generally thought to affect play, relatively little attention has been paid to the meaning of specific toys in children's lives (Sutton-Smith 1986). Garvey (1990) observes that certain objects may have strong, private emotional appeal. These favorite toys are incorporated into the child's expressive behavior, providing the means by which the child can represent or express feelings, concerns, or preoccupying interests. Sutton-Smith (1986) goes further to suggest that the passionate attachment to a toy may be critical to the construction of the mind of the explorer, imaginer, player, or daydreamer. He cites numerous examples from interviews with adults suggesting a relation between the favorite toys of childhood and adult interests. One mathematics professor at the Massachusetts Institute of Technology described a strong emotional attachment to gears in early childhood.

Garvey (1990) describes gender differences in preferences for toys in freely chosen activities in nursery schools. For example, boys cluster at the tool bench or push trucks around the room, and girls gather in the kitchen corner to cook and wash dishes. Similarly, Paley (1984) comments upon gender differences in preschool children's toy preferences. Rheingold and

Cook (1975) argue that such gender differences have their origins in parental practices. They inventoried the contents of the bedrooms of children under six years of age. In terms of props for pretend play, boys were provided with more vehicles, toy animals, depots, machines, and military toys. Girls were provided with more dolls, doll houses, and domestic toys. Although boys' rooms contained some dolls (e.g., cowboys), virtually none represented females or babies. There were no differences between the boys' and girls' rooms in respect to the presence of stuffed animals. Rheingold and Cook conclude that parents were not simply acceding to the preexisting interests of their children, but were themselves responsible for creating the different sets of objects found in boys' and girls' bedrooms. It is unclear, however, the extent to which young boys and girls choose different toys to incorporate into their spontaneous pretend play at home.

The Locations of Everyday Pretending

Systematic studies of the physical locale of everyday pretending are practically nonexistent. Indeed, with the exception of Sanders and Harper's (1976) study of pretending indoors versus outdoors within a preschool, almost no attention has been paid to the typical locations of children's spontaneous pretend play.

Distribution of Pretending Across the Observation Sessions

If children's pretend play is related to the social context, as is suggested in chapter 4, then it is important to consider the extent to which it is affected by the presence of an observer. However, very little is known about the basic methodological issue of the length of time needed to obtain an adequate sample of pretend play at various ages and in various contexts. Manwell and Mengert (1934) made five separate twenty-minute observations of the same children in a preschool classroom and found considerable variation across observations in the amount of pretending that occurred. Most research on children's play is based on relatively brief time samples lasting from a few minutes (e.g. O'Connell and Bretherton 1984) to one hour (e.g. Dunn and Wooding 1977).

Data Analysis

Objects Used in Pretending

We first determined whether or not an object was involved in the episode, and then categorized the objects into several types. An object had to be incorporated into the pretending to be counted in this analysis; objects that were thrown aside or moved from place to place were excluded. For each of the following categories of objects, we measured the length of time in which that category of object was used and then computed the percentage of total play time involving that category. Note that we double coded those instances in which objects from different categories were used simultaneously. For example, if the child created a five-minute scenario using a toy car (replica object) and a pencil (substitute object) as a wrench for repairing the engine, both the replica-object category and the substitute-object category were credited with five minutes.

Real object. A real object is an ordinary object that is incorporated into the play in a conventional way. For example, a child enacts eating imaginary food from a real spoon. Note that simply putting the spoon into the mouth does not count as pretending unless it is accompanied by nonverbal enactment (e.g. eating noises), verbal enactment (e.g. "Mm. This cake tastes good") or other pretend comment (e.g. "Let's pretend that we're eating").

Substitute object. A substitute object is an object that is referred to or treated as another object. For example, five-year-old Rachael informed her three-year-old sister, Molly, "This [toy comb] is my cheese cracker." She then pretended to eat the "cheese cracker."

Replica object. A replica object is a realistic miniature of an object that is used conventionally during play. For example, a toy car pushed back and forth to accompanying sound effects is a "replica object," while the same car used as an airplane is a "substitute object." Note that we were conservative in attributing pretend play to children's conventional actions on replica objects. Simply using an object in a manner suggested by its physical characteristics, e.g., pushing a toy car with wheels, without clear gestures of enactment or transformational talk, was not considered to be pretending and hence is excluded from this analysis. Similarly, the appropriate use of child-sized miniatures, e.g., playing basketball on a miniature basketball court, was not included unless accompanied by enactment.

Constructed object. A constructed object is constructed by the child out of play dough, blocks, cookie dough, etc. prior to being incorporated into the pretense.

Settings and costumes. Settings and costumes provide a background appropriate to the play. For example, a bed is used as a stage, or an article of clothing or other object appropriate to the enacted role is worn or draped over the body during play. Although objects used as settings or costumes may be real, substitute, replica, or constructed, they are actively manipulated only while setting the stage for the enactment.

Locations for Pretending

Although parts of some observation sessions were conducted outside of the home, most of the observations were made within the home itself. In this analysis we categorized pretending in terms of the rooms in which it occurred. We then calculated the percentage of play time spent in each location. Note that a single episode of play may involve more than one location, e.g., the play begins in the livingroom and continues in the bedroom.

Distribution of Pretending Across the Observation Sessions

Observation sessions typically began in the morning around breakfast time. Occasionally, the observation session began after the child's afternoon nap, but these afternoon observations were distributed equally across the age range. Not all children were observed for a full four hours at each data point, so only episodes within the first three hours of observation were analyzed. A full three hours of observation was not available for five children at twelve months and for one child at twenty-four months. Therefore, this analysis begins with eight children at twenty-four months and continues with all nine children at thirty-six and forty-eight months. The measure of occurrence is "duration." "Duration" refers to the length of episodes beginning within each hour. Play is considered to "occur" within the hour in which it began. Thus, if an episode of pretend play crossed hourly boundaries, e.g., began in hour two and ended in hour three, it was considered to have occurred in hour two.

Results

What Kinds of Objects Do Children Use When Pretending?

We first determined the mean percentage of episodes involving one or more objects. We found that across the age range pretending occurred predominantly with objects. A mean percentage of 100 percent (± 0 percent), 80 percent (± 5), 86 percent (± 3), and 79 percent (± 6) of episodes of pretend play involved objects at twelve, twenty-four, thirty-six, and forty-eight months, respectively. Figure 8.1 summarizes the mean percentage of children's total pretend play time involving various categories of objects. (This analysis also was conducted using episodes as the unit of analysis and comparable results were obtained.) (See Haight 1989.) Across the age range, children pretended predominantly with replica objects, and every child pretended with replica objects during at least part of every observation session. A repeated measures ANOVA revealed a significant change in the mean percentage of pretending in-

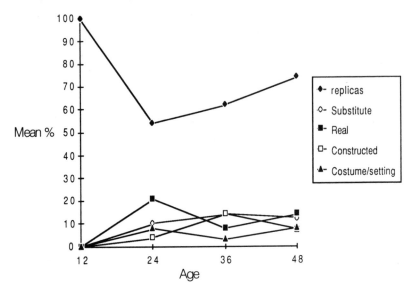

Figure 8.1 The mean percentage of total pretend play time involving various categories of objects.

volving replica objects across the age range, F (3, 19) = 3.20, $p.$ < 0.05. Any pretending that occurred at twelve months involved replica objects exclusively, with somewhat lower levels occurring at subsequent ages. Nevertheless, although children incorporated other categories of objects into their play as early as twenty-four months (including substitute objects by five children), replica objects were the most frequently occurring category of objects throughout the age range. Among the other categories of objects, no single category ever accounted for more than a mean of 21 percent of the play time.

What Kind of Replica Objects Do Children Use, and Are There Developmental Changes?

We next listed the replica objects with which each child pretended at each age level. Table 8.1 lists the replicas with which more than one child pretended at any given age level. Across the age levels, the categories of replicas pretended with by the most children were stuffed animals (eight children), and cars and trucks (eight children). At twelve months, three of the four children who pretended used stuffed animals. At twenty-four months, many categories of replica objects were observed. This is the only age, however, at which children (three) pretended with shopping carts. At thirty-six months, we observed children pretending with Barbie dolls and this play continued through forty-eight months.

Is There Individual Stability in the Use of Particular Types of Replicas Across Development?

Table 8.1 also shows individual stability in the types of replicas with which various children pretended. Each of the nine children pretended at more than one observation with at least one type of replica toy. Charlie pretended at twenty-four, thirty-six, and forty-eight months with "other miniature animates and accessories" including replica zoo, pirate, and "Wild West" sets. At twenty-four and forty-eight months he pretended with Superhero action figures, and with cars and trucks. Elizabeth pretended at twenty-four, thirty-six, and forty-eight months

Table 8.1.
Children pretending with various types of replicas
Age in months

Replicas[a]	12	24	36	48
Stuffed animals	John, Kathy, Nancy	John, Kathy, Charlie, Elizabeth	John, Justin, Joe, Nancy	Justin, Joe, Molly
Barbie dolls and accessories	—	—	Kathy, Molly	Kathy, Molly, Nancy
Baby dolls and accessories	—	Elizabeth, Molly	Elizabeth	Elizabeth
Child dolls	—	—	Justin, John, Molly	—
Action figures	—	Charlie, Joe, Michael	—	Charlie, Joe, Michael
Cars, trucks, heavy equipment	—	Charlie, John, Joe, Elizabeth, Molly, Nancy	Charlie, John, Joe, Justin, Michael	Michael, Justin
Train sets	—	—	Charlie, Justin, John	—
Other vehicles (boats, planes, buses, etc.)	—	Joe, Michael	Joe, Michael, Justin, John	Charlie, Nancy
Other miniature animates and accessories	—	Elizabeth, Charlie, Joe	Charlie, Joe, Michael, John	Charlie, Joe, Michael, Justin
Instruments	—	—	Charlie, John	—
Puppets	—	Molly	Kathy, Nancy	—
Shopping cart	—	Elizabeth, Molly, Joe	—	—

Table 8.1 (cont'd).

Dishes	—	Joe	Elizabeth, Kathy, Molly, Joe	—

[a] Objects listed represent replicas pretended with by two or more children at any given age.

with baby dolls and their various accessories, including miniature blankets and a cradle. Justin pretended with stuffed animals at thirty-six and forty-eight months, and for extended periods of time with "cars, trucks, and heavy equipment," including bulldozers, dump trucks, cranes, garbage trucks, and steam rollers. John pretended at twelve, twenty-four, and thirty-six months with stuffed animals, including his baby brother's monkey. He pretended at twenty-four and thirty-six months with cars and trucks. Joe pretended at twenty-four, thirty-six, and forty-eight months with "other miniature animates and accessories"—a replica house with people and animals. He also pretended at twenty-four and forty-eight months with Superhero action figures, at twenty-four and thirty-six months with cars and trucks and other vehicles, and, briefly, at thirty-six and forty-eight months with stuffed animals (a monkey and a "Sesame Street" character). At twelve and twenty-four months Kathy pretended with stuffed animals including a monkey and Disney characters. At thirty-six and forty-eight months, Kathy pretended extensively with several Barbie dolls. At thirty-six and forty-eight months Molly also pretended extensively with several Barbie dolls and their numerous accessories including combs, clothes, and jewelry. Michael pretended with action figures at twenty-four and forty-eight months including Batman and Captain America. At thirty-six and forty-eight months he pretended with "other miniature animates and accessories" including a hospital, fire station and replica Sesame Street. He also pretended with cars and trucks at thirty-six and forty-eight months, and with other vehicles including a bus and boat at twenty-four and thirty-six months. Nancy pretended with various stuffed animals at twelve and thirty-six months.

Are There Gender Differences in the Replica Objects with which Boys and Girls Pretend?

Table 8.1 also suggests gender differences in the use of replicas during pretend play. First, all four girls pretended with dolls. Three girls pretended with Barbies, at both thirty-six and forty-eight months, and two girls pretended with girl baby dolls. In contrast, no boy pretended with a female doll. Four of the five boys did pretend with stuffed animals and two with little boy dolls. In addition, three boys pretended with Superhero action figures at two age levels. No girls pretended with action figures or male dolls.

Gender differences are also suggested in vehicle play. At twenty-four months, three boys and three girls pretended with cars and trucks. At thirty-six and forty-eight months, however, no girls pretended with cars and trucks. All five boys pretended with cars and trucks at thirty-six months, and two continued this play at forty-eight months. Further, only boys (three) pretended with train sets. All five boys pretended with "other vehicles," and one girl, Nancy, pretended with a plane.

Interestingly, more boys than girls pretended with "other miniature animates and accessories." These included fire stations, zoos, hospitals, houses, and farms. All five boys pretended with these toys, and four pretended with them at two or three age levels. Only one girl pretended with a farm, and she did so at the youngest age level (twenty-four months) for which pretend with this category of replicas was observed.

How Many Families Set Aside Special Rooms in Their Homes for Play?

All of the children in our study had special space within the home to play. Two of the children had their own bedrooms and the other seven shared a bedroom with a sibling. In addition, the families of four children set aside special rooms, "playrooms" or "toyrooms," in their homes for the purpose of play. Although bedrooms and playrooms were the official location for play materials, toys used in pretend play typically were distributed throughout the house including livingrooms, in which all of the children pretended.

Where Do Children Pretend?

Figure 8.2 summarizes the mean percent of children's play time occurring in various locations. From the onset of pretend play at twelve months, children played in a variety of locations, but most commonly in livingrooms/playrooms. A repeated measures ANOVA revealed no significant change in the extent to which children played in livingrooms/playrooms.

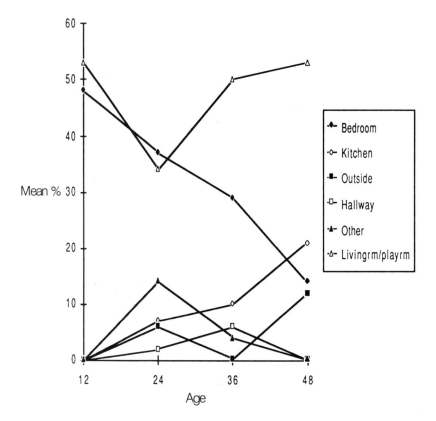

Figure 8.2 The mean percentage of children's pretend play time in various locations from 12 to 48 months

When Does Pretending Occur Within the Observation Session?

Figure 8.3 summarizes the percentage of children's play time beginning in the first three hours of observation from twenty-four to forty-eight months. A repeated measures ANOVA revealed a significant change in the percentage of pretending that occurred in the first hour of observation, F (2, 19) = 3.92, $p <$ 0.04. At twenty-four months, the bulk of children's pretend play occurred in the first hour of observation, and very little occurred in the third hour of observation. By contrast, at thirty-six and forty-eight months, the bulk of pretending occurred in the third hour of observation, and relatively little occurred in the first hour. The percentage of episodes beginning in hour two remained relatively stable throughout the age range.

Examination of when the longest episodes occurred parallel the above findings. At twenty-four months, the longest episode for seven children occurred in the first hour. At thirty-six and forty-eight months, however, the longest episodes occurred in the second and third hours for eight and nine children, respectively.

Discussion

From within the vantage point of mainstream culture, the practices of equipping young children with objects specialized for use in pretend play and setting aside locations specifically for play are easily taken for granted. Yet these practices point to a potentially powerful indirect route by which caregivers influence pretending. Caregivers' role as providers of props and locations for pretending is analytically separate from, but potentially as important as, their role as play partners. These practices also communicate beliefs that pretend play is an appropriate and valued activity.

Objects

All of the children in our study had large collections of replica objects intended for use in pretend play. In contrast, Whiting and Edwards (1988) observed that with the exception of the children within their American community, and a few children from wealthy and modern families within other cultural communities, children of the world generally do not own toys. Rogoff (personal communication, 1992) observed that the practice of toy ownership is limited in rural Guatemala, with children typically possessing zero to three toys. Similarly, toys are extremely rare in Swaziland (Trousdale, personal communication, 1992), and young middle-class Italian children typically are not provided with toys, at least not during infancy (New 1982). Note that these children may play with other objects, and

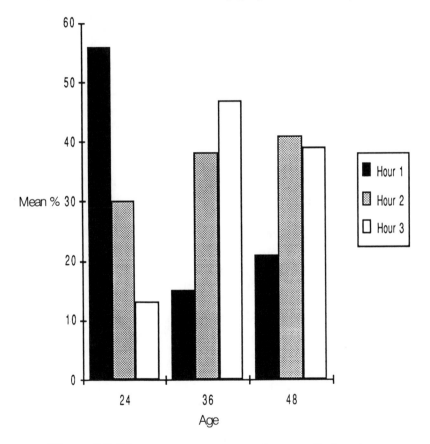

Figure 8.3 The mean percentage of pretend play time beginning in hours one to three from 24 to 48 months

their parents' interest or disinterest in play may be reflected in ways other than the provision of special toys.

Our results corroborate earlier research indicating that very young children from Western communities use realistic objects in their play and that they begin to substitute one object for another toward the end of the second year (e.g., Piaget 1962; see Rubin, Fein, and Vandenberg 1983 for review). Our results expand these findings by revealing that within the home children pretended predominantly with realistic objects throughout the age range—long past the point at which they became able to pretend with substitute objects. Indeed, at forty-eight months replica objects accounted for 74 percent of their pretend play at home. In contrast, Schwartzman (1986) found that 75 percent of pretend play events in preschool involved the use of blocks rather than the more structured and seemingly realistic doll house materials. One possible explanation for the difference between our findings and those of Schwartzman is that children's own collections of replica toys contain a greater variety of toys which appeal to them personally than do the more generic collections found in preschool.

These findings also suggest that the function of realistic objects may change as children mature. According to Vygotsky (1978), children initially require the use of realistic pivots in order to pretend. Perhaps as they develop, such realistic props are no longer necessary for symbolic thought, but, as Newson and Newson (1979) suggested, provide the reference points from which imagination ranges, allowing more subtle and complicated pretending to occur. In the later preschool years replica objects may also provide touchstones of peer culture, resources not so much provided by parents as demanded by children and around which they and their friends create and sustain shared meanings.

Our results also suggest that there are gender differences in the replica objects with which boys and girls pretend. Given the small sample size, however, future research employing a larger sample size should be conducted and supplemented with inventories of toy collections provided by parents. In general, girls pretended with baby dolls and Barbies while boys pretended with action figures and vehicles. These findings suggest that the cultural nature of pretend play is reflected not only in differences across cultural communities, but within communities in the toys given to and appropriated by young boys and girls. Such gender differences in toy purchases and use reflect cultural notions of gender appropriateness.

Although adults may shape children's pretend play through the objects they provide for play and the beliefs they communicate regarding gender-appropriate play, children's unique individual preferences and interests are reflected in those objects they appropriate for play. Our results indicate that all of the children pretended with a particular replica for a one-year period, and several children pretended with the same replica for at least two years. Future research should probe further the significance of particular toys in the lives of individual children.

Locations of Pretend Play

We also discovered that there was a social dimension to the locations in which children typically pretended. Throughout the age range pretend play occurred primarily in communal rooms, particularly livingrooms, playrooms, and kitchens. Pretending seemed to flourish when other people were nearby—available for recruitment as play partners, engaged in activities that could be converted into pretense, or simply comfortably and unobtrusively present as the child pretended alone.

Just as the practice of supplying young children with special toys reflects cultural values about play, so does setting aside special locations for play. All of the children within our study had their own bedrooms for the storage and use of play materials, and some families even set aside entire rooms solely for the purpose of play. In contrast, Guatemalan families do not set aside special spaces for play (Rogoff, personal communication, 1992). Similarly, the Taiwanese families studied by Fung did not have playrooms within their homes (personal communication, 1991). Note that this does not necessarily mean that the families in Rogoff's and Fung's studies did not value their children's play. In less affluent communities or in heavily populated areas with limited availability of living space, parental values concerning play may be expressed in other ways.

Occurrence of Pretend Play Within the Observation Episodes

Our final analysis of the physical conditions for everyday pretending focused on when pretending occurred within the observation session. Was pretending evenly distributed across the several hours of observation or did pretending occur more frequently at certain times? We found that at twenty-four months most of the pretending occurred in the first hour of observation, but at thirty-six and forty-eight months a different pattern emerged: the bulk of children's play occurred in the second and third hours of observation. In addition, the longest episodes tended to occur later. These longer episodes may be more elaborate or complex than earlier episodes and hence represent children's most competent performances.

Developmental changes in the distribution of children's play within the observation periods have important implications for sampling, calling into question the ecological validity of studies that encompass only brief periods of observation. Younger children's tendency to play towards the beginning of the observation period may reflect an interaction between their alertness/fatigue and how cognitively taxing they find play. In addition, as children develop, their pretend play may become more susceptible to external disturbances necessitating changes in observation procedures. It is unclear, however, what type of changes may be needed as there were at least two probable sources of external disturbance in the present study. First, because the observation periods were so long, the observer typically arrived just as the child was waking up in the morning. Younger children may more easily fit their brief, simple pretend episodes around caregiving routines such as toileting, dressing, eating, etc. Older children may require more extended periods of uninterrupted time to elaborate their themes satisfactorily. Second, older children may be more self-conscious in the presence of an observer, necessitating longer periods of habituation. This second factor reminds us that one consequence of children's growing understanding of self and other is that they may come to interpret differently the social situation of being observed.

9

A Summary of Major Findings: Portraits of Kathy and Charlie

Up to this point we have presented our findings in a piecemeal fashion, one topic at a time. This chapter will integrate these main findings through the presentation of the pretend play of one little girl, Kathy, and one little boy, Charlie. In addition, these descriptions will illustrate how personalities, individual interests, and relationships are expressed through pretend play. Kathy, Charlie, and their mothers were neither the most nor the least prolific and imaginative pretenders. They were chosen because they represent somewhat contrasting family constellations and child interests.

Kathy's Pretend Play

During the first two years of the study, Kathy lived with her parents and sister Susan, four and a half years older, in a high rise apartment in urban Chicago. As was true for many children in this study, the urban environment and relatively severe weather combined to keep Kathy indoors with her mother much of the time. Her mother, Priscilla, who had worked as an elementary school teacher, felt strongly that she needed to be with her children full time until they reached school age. Since Susan was at school until midafternoons, and Kathy's father, a businessman, was rarely at home during weekdays, Priscilla was Kathy's primary companion, caregiver, and teacher. In addition, we observed Kathy pretending with a same-aged friend and with her sister, with whom she shared an affectionate and supportive relationship.

As a toddler, Kathy experienced considerable encouragement of pretend play. When she was twelve months old, Priscilla directed pretend play to Kathy on five occasions during the two-hour observation. She pretended to eat Kathy's legs as she changed her diapers, suggested that Kathy drive the family car as they waited to pick up Susan at school, greeted "Mr. Bear (a stuffed toy)," and inquired whether Kathy was going to school as she carried around her sister's lunchbox. The only pretending that Kathy engaged in during the twelve-month observation occurred during play with her mother. In the following segment from the transcript Kathy displays her emerging ability to treat objects nonliterally— hugging her stuffed monkey:

(Kathy and her mother are in the livingroom. Kathy is fussing.)
    M. Kathy. Look at George. (M. holding stuffed monkey on her lap facing outwards.)
    K. (looks)
    M. Come here. Come over here and see George.
    K. (vocalizes)
    M. Here's George.
    K. (walks towards M.)
    M. Kathy. Look.
    K. (hugs monkey)
    M. Come here, George. Oh, hi. (As K. hugging.)
    M. Hi Georgie. (As K. carries monkey away towards TV.)

This episode illustrates a pretend activity that mothers commonly engaged in with twelve month olds, namely, treating a stuffed toy as if it were real. In an attempt to entertain a bored and cranky child, Priscilla drew Kathy's attention to the stuffed monkey. As Kathy hugged the monkey, Priscilla added appropriate, nonliteral talk.

At twenty-four months, Priscilla continued to serve as Kathy's primary pretend play partner. Indeed, 97 percent of Kathy's pretend play occurred with her mother. Kathy particularly enjoyed stories about princesses, and the majority of her pretend play centered on Cinderella. Priscilla supported this pretend play indirectly by providing her daughter with a handmade Cinderella cape and skirt. She also supplied further information with which to elaborate the pretense during discussions of related real-life events, such as the the babysitter's upcoming high school prom. "... Lorie's. . . gonna wear a dress like Cinderella to the prom, isn't she? She's gonna have a, a person who's dressed like—almost like a prince come and pick her up. And they're going to go dance . . ." Priscilla also supported Kathy's pretend play directly. For example, in the following excerpt, Priscilla gamely assumed the role of prince to Kathy's Cinderella.

(Kathy and her mother are in Kathy's bedroom. Mother is putting on Kathy's Cinderella costume.)
M. Oh look how beautiful. (M. pulls skirt down, adjusts and smoothes skirt.)
M. And here you are Cinderella with your cape on. (M. takes cape off hanger and puts it around K.'s shoulders.)
K. Cape on.
M. Pretend you're at the ball. How would you dance?
K. Dance. Like that. (K. turns and jumps a few times.)
M. Oh how beautiful. Dance some more.
K. No.
M. No?
K. Dance Prince.
M. You want to dance with the Prince? Well, I don't know where the. . . Where's the Prince?
K. That ballroom.
M. He's at the ballroom.
K. Go ballroom.
M. Let's pretend this is the ballroom. And I'll be the Prince, alright? . . . Let's dance. (M. and K. hold hands and sway, etc. M. sings, "dododo.")
K. Dance Prince.
M. I'm the Prince. Do I look like the Prince?
K. No. (M. laughs.)

As this episode illustrates, Priscilla asked questions which prompted the appropriate enactment from Kathy ("How

would you dance?"), and elaborated Kathy's pretend contributions ("Where's the Prince?"). For her part, Kathy spontaneously contributed verbal transformations elaborating the
Cinderella theme (e.g., "Dance Prince"). Interestingly, Priscilla
was more likely than the other mothers to produce role transformations ("I'll be the Prince"), and other explicit pretend
markers ("Pretend you're at the ball."). Kathy was the only
child in the sample who spontaneously produced an explicit
role transformation at twenty-four months. During a ride in the
elevator subsequent to the above episode, Kathy announced,
"I'm Cinderella." This raises the question of whether Priscilla's
frequent metacommunications during pretend play facilitated
Kathy's early acquisition of explicit role transformations.

At thirty-six months, Kathy's pretend play remained predominantly social (93 percent of pretend play time), and her
mother continued to serve as her primary play partner (89
percent of social pretend play). However, she also pretended
with other familiar people. Her interest in princesses shifted to
Barbie dolls, which became the center of her pretend world.
Priscilla provided her with numerous Barbie dolls and their
accessories and discussed the difference between make-believe
and real. She participated directly in Kathy's pretend play by
good-humoredly enduring Kathy's pretend manicures and by
discussing the likes and dislikes of Kathy's "Diva" doll and the
fears of her play dough animals. In the following excerpt Kathy
and her mother make an elaborate imaginary birthday cake
with pink frosting.

(K has been pretending alone with two Barbie dolls, a
dancer and a smaller girl.)
K. You little. I'm big. (K holds the dancer doll above the
little girl doll. Then K makes the little girl doll address the
dancer doll.)
K. Maybe you're . . . Maybe it isn't my birthday. (K
walks over to M. She holds dolls upright in front of her
face, facing outwards to M., and makes the little girl doll
address M.)
K. How do I, how do you decorate our cake?

M. Well, what do you like to put on your cake? (To little girl doll.)

K. Umm. Ah. (Wandering around holding dolls.)

K. But we don't have any frosting. (As holding up dolls to address M.)

M. Why don't you make some? (To dolls.)

K. How? . . .

M. . . . Kathy could make you some . . . (To dolls.)

K. But we need some . . . (Wanders over to table.)

M. Well, I found some. (Gestures as if picking something up. Then gestures as if stirring what she picked up.) Here's some frosting. This is white. Do you want to make it different colors?

M. (Holds fist out to K.)

K. (Holds dolls over M.'s fist.)

M. What colors are you making?

K. Blue. (K. making dolls stir imaginary frosting.)

M. Blue? What else?

K. Red and purple for you.

M. Oh.

K. (Stops making doll stir. M. still holding out fist.)

K. Here. (Holds doll up to M. as if doll is giving M. the bowl of frosting.)

M. Now should I make a cake?

K. Yeah.

M. . . . Here's the cake. I'm making it. (As she makes stirring gestures.)

K. But you have to put sugar into it so it tastes good. (K. has put the dolls down and wandered over to the table.)

M. Sugar? What else do you put into a cake? You come put in the sugar. (Holding hands out for cake bowl.)

K. (Walks towards M. then stops and looks around.) You can decorate it like—(Picks up a pillow and shakes it. K. is speaking for herself now.)

M. (Watches, smiling.)

K. You put—decorate like this. (K. continues shaking the pillow.)

M. What else do you put?

K. Frosting.

M. Frosting. What else?
K. Flow, flowers. That taste good. (Puts pillow back on couch.)
   M. (Laughs.)
M. How about a little vanilla?
K. Yeah.
M. Here comes your song. (On the tape player.)
(K. dances to birthday song and sings. She picks up the dolls and continues dancing around the room.)

As this excerpt illustrates, Kathy's ability to pretend continued to grow between twenty-four and thirty-six months. By thirty-six months, Kathy's pretend play was more sustained, she was able to enact both parts of an imaginary dialogue and to pretend with objects that were completely imaginary (e.g., blue frosting). Although these developing skills, as well as our other observations of her, suggest that Kathy has the competence to pretend alone, she continued to seek her mother's participation, and Priscilla continued to respond to Kathy's initiations in a supportive and interested manner.

By the time Kathy was forty-eight months, her family had moved into a large two-story house with a fenced-in backyard in a nearby suburb. Her pretend play remained predominantly social (72 percent), but Priscilla was no longer her primary pretend play partner (only 17 percent of social pretend play). Kathy played most frequently with her older sister, Susan, who was unusually warm and tolerant of her little sister, skillfully incorporating her into her own pretend play. Kathy's pretend play continued to revolve around her collection of Barbie dolls and accessories. The sisters engaged in lengthy episodes (up to forty minutes) of pretending involving the adventures of several Barbie dolls who went to school, played guitar, got lost, and fell into dark holes only to be rescued by an imaginary dragon with purple spots. (See chapter 3, introductory example.) In addition, Priscilla had begun inviting neighborhood children to the house to play with Kathy. As the following excerpt illustrates, at forty-eight months, Kathy was learning to negotiate pretend play with a peer.

(Kathy and her four-year-old friend, Jackie, are playing on a screened-in porch while Priscilla reads on a nearby couch. K. is sitting on a lawn chair and J. is standing facing K. holding a large ball.)

K. I'm a store manager. (To Jackie.) Hi what would you like to buy? OK that will be fifteen cents and one fifteen cents. That will be fifteen cents and a ten dollars.

J. I don't really want to buy anything. . . .

K. OK. Here. Oh here's your check. (K. makes quick motions with her hand as if working a cash register.)

J. Thank you. (J. takes imaginary paper from K.) Pretend I don't buy anything.

K. OK.

J. Pretend I don't buy anything. . . .

K. Jackie it's my turn cause um I didn't really have much things but balls. (K. gets up from her chair and walks toward J. who is riding the trike.) Jackie my turn. (J. stops the trike, gets off it, and then gets on the car. K. gets on the trike. They both ride around on porch.)

K. I need to go to the store. Ahuh. (K. and J. are still riding around in circles. K. hums a song. Then K. leaves J. on the patio and goes into the playroom where M. is sitting.)

M. Why don't you play house, this is a good chance to. Or why don't you two go bake me some muffins in the stove and set up a bakery or something.

K. Maybe I'll cook the . . . and way over here. (K. walks into next room then returns.)

M. OK but you do it outside with Jackie, OK.

K. But I want to pretend with you.

M. (Laughs.) But that would leave Jackie out. How 'bout why don't you two pretend you're making a pie like the pie makers. . .

As this excerpt illustrates, although Kathy was capable of pretending with a peer, Priscilla continued to offer assistance. When other children were available, however, she directed and coached Kathy to pretend with them. When other children were not available, Priscilla continued to serve as a pretend partner for Kathy.

Charlie's Pretend Play

Charlie lived in an apartment in a college dormitory where his parents were employed as residents' advisors while Charlie's father pursued a graduate degree in social work. Like Kathy, Charlie spent long periods of time indoors with his mother. Sandy was a social worker who continued to work several hours a week after Charlie was born. She felt, however, that it was important to stay home during Charlie's early years and she was his primary companion and caregiver. Unlike the other children in the study, Charlie was an only child and was never observed playing with other children. Both of Charlie's parents, however, were interested in his play and frequently entered into his pretend world, creating make-believe parades, going camping, and finding pirates' treasure.

At twelve months, Charlie, like three of the other children in our study, did not pretend during the observations. As the following excerpt illustrates, however, his mother did direct pretend play to him.

(Charlie and his mother are in the livingroom. C. is fussing. M. picks up C. and sets him down in front of toys.)

M. Want to look at the train? (As she moves train back and forth.) Look. Who's on the train? (Fisher-Price person.) Huh?

(C. continues fussing.) . . . Charlie. Charlie, look at the train! Woo, woo, woo, woo, woo, woo . . . (M. pushes train.)

C. (Quiets, then grabs for train.)

M. (Pushes train forward.)

(C. pulls train backwards. They repeat these actions several times until C. throws himself at M. and begins fussing.)

In this episode, Sandy initiates pretend play with the cranky Charlie in an apparent attempt to entertain him. She suggests that someone is on the train ("*Who's* on the train?" not "*What's* on the train?"), and treats the train as if it were real by making sound effects while pushing it. She not only draws Charlie's attention to the train ("Charlie, Charlie look at the train"), but supports him at a level appropriate to his ability, modelling the action of pulling the train. The interest in trains exhibited by this mother-child pair in the early episode carried over into their later pretense (see chapter 6, example 2).

At twenty-four months, all of Charlie's pretend play occurred with his mother. The following example is typical in that it revolves around his stuffed bear. His other preferred toy at this age was a replica zoo set, complete with miniature train.

> M. Oh, look at the little bear. Little bear. (As M. cradles bear in arms like infant.)
> C. (Takes bear from M. and carries it towards rocking chair.)
> M. Oh, is he gonna sit in the chair?
> C. Sit in chair.
> M. OK. Uhoh. (As bear falls out of chair. C puts back.) There's the bear.
> C. Rock. (Standing in front of chair rocking bear.)
> M. He's sitting in the chair. Rock, rock. Back and forth.
> C. (Still rocking bear who is sitting in rocking chair facing outwards.)
> M. He's gonna hold on? (As C. is straightening bear's sitting position.)
> M. Well he's only gonna hold onto one side here. He's not big enough to hold onto both. Just hold onto one side.
> C. (Hands M. the bear and then a book.)
> M. You want me to read the bear a book? It says, "Caps for sale."
> C. A bear. (As putting a miniature robot, or "Gobot," in bear's lap.)
> M. The bear have the Gobot? OK. Bear will hold the Gobot. OK.
> C. Bear. Gobot.
> M. The bear has the Gobot.

In this episode Charlie's mother produced enactments (cradling bear in arms like an infant) and prompted and elaborated on Charlie's contributions. Charlie introduced several ideas of his own (rocking the bear, giving the bear a Gobot) but provided only brief verbal comments. Moreover, most of his verbalizations ("Sit on chair." "A bear." "Bear. Gobot.") were reproductions of his mother's detailed commentary on his own pretend actions. Thus, at this age, Charlie and his mother jointly created pretend scenarios but Charlie contributed relatively little to the verbalization of pretend transformations.

At thirty-six months and forty-eight months, Charlie's mother remained his primary play partner. Unlike the other children in the study, Charlie was relatively isolated from peers. Perhaps as a consequence, he produced more solitary pretense and less role playing. At thirty-six months, for example, he engaged in an episode of solitary pretending that lasted twenty-one minutes. Despite this, most of his pretend play was social and involved extensive use of miniature replicas, including the zoo set and, as illustrated below, "Wild West" and pirate sets. The following example occurred at forty-eight months:

(Charlie and his mother are seated in the livingroom enacting a treasure hunt.)
M.   Wow! Look at that treasure. Wow! Where did it come from? (Speaking in a higher voice, for little man on a horse which she faces outwards towards the ship.)
C.   Well, it was in the treasure chest.
M.   Whose treasure chest does it belong to?
C.   It might be that naughty pirate's!
M.   You think it's his?
C.   Yeah. But we can't [unintelligible].
M.   What if he comes over?
C.   He's not gonna come over.
M.   Oh no! (As she moves pirate on horse over to treasure.)
C.   No! You play this game wrong.
M.   Oh, that's not how you play it? OK. He'll stay over here then. (Walks pirate on horse away.)
C.   He has cage on him, so he can't get away. Because— everyone has cage on him because they don't want him to go away!
M.   Mmmmm. Patches is hungry. He's eating his food. (Makes horse eat, accompanied by eating noises.)
C.   He is hungry also. (Holds up other horse with rider.)

M. Are you hungry from your long trip. (Addressing Charlie's horse.)

C. Yeah. I'm gonna take a rest on the horse feeder. (Talking for horse. Smiles up at M. as he puts horse on feeder.)

M. You're going to have a rest on the horse feeder! Oh no! You knocked over the horse feeding trough. Here you go. (Stands up corral.)

C. Don't worry. I'm magic. (For horse, animated intonation.)

M. You're magic? I'm gonna go in the fence here. (As she moves horse into corral.)

C. Look, more food! (To horse as he places it in corral.)

M. Oh, good. Thank you. Mmm. This is good food. (Makes eating noises for horse.)

C. Is that enough?

M. Yes.

M. What kind of food was he eating?

C. He was eating rice and pork chops.

M. Rice and pork chops. Mmmmm.

C. And lots of biscuits.

M. Biscuits!

C. Yeah.

M. Ohhhhh. Do you think horses eat biscuits?

C. No!!

M. What do you think horses eat?

C. Hay and milk and butter.

M. Hay and milk and butter? (C. and M. laughing.) All those things.

C. Yeah. Hay and milk and butter.

M. Hay and milk and butter. Is that—what are you gonna have for your lunch?

M. and C. together: Hay and milk and butter! (Laugh.)

M. Should I give you hay—hay sandwich?

C. Yeah. Give me a hay sandwich. (As he holds out hand.)

M. (M. slaps C.'s hand as if giving something.)

C. Yuck. (After he puts his hand to mouth. Then spits.)

M. Oh don't spit that's not nice. Yuck.

C. I was spitting out the hay.

M. Yeah but you don't—you're just pretending so you don't really want to spit. Yuck.

C. Hey, you want to have a hay sandwich. (After he picks up person, addressing M.'s person.)

M. I would like a hay sandwich. I like hay sandwiches. (In high voice as he holds up person.)

C. Was that the horse?

M. Yes. (Laughs.) Do horses really—

C. Here's two more hay sandwiches. (Gestures as if giving to horse.)

M. Oh, you knocked me over. (High voice.)

(The episodes continues in this vein for several more minutes.)

This episode illustrates four-year-old Charlie's continued enjoyment and elaboration of pretend play with his mother as well as his mother's involvement as a full participant. Sandy acts not only as a commentator on Charlie's play but enters the pretend world in the roles of treasure hunter and horse. Charlie exhibits a much firmer command of the language of pretend play than he did in the earlier example. And he exercises much more control or authorship of the episode, introducing pretend transformations ("He was eating rice and pork chops."), criticizing his mother's rendition ("No! You play this game wrong.") and responding serenely to exigencies as they arise ("Don't worry. I'm magic."). Within the context of ongoing pretend interactions with his mother, he has emerged as a skillful and imaginative pretender who jokes with his partner about hay sandwiches.

Conclusion

These individual portaits of Kathy and Charlie serve several functions. First, they illustrate how the main outlines of our findings apply to two very different children. Throughout the age range, both Kathy's and Charlie's pretend play was predominantly social. Like the other children in this study, their pretend play was responsive to the interested involvement of other, more experienced pretenders, usually their mothers. Both mothers introduced the pretend mode to their children by twelve months and by twenty-four months the children actively initiated pretend play with their mothers. In the earliest years, Kathy and Charlie reproduced their mothers' pretend suggestions and incorporated them into their subsequent play. Throughout the age range, Kathy's and Charlie's mothers supported their children's pretend play directly through prompting and elaborations of their pretend contributions and indirectly through the physical context that they created. Kathy and Charlie pretended primarily with replica toys. By the time Kathy's family moved to the suburbs, their home included a playroom and Kathy's mother encouraged social pretense by hosting other children from the neighborhood.

These portraits also reflect the expression of one little girl's and one little boy's individual interests, preoccupations, and unique family situations. Kathy pretended most extensively and intently with her Barbie dolls. This interest remained strong for at least a full year and may be related to her earlier interest in Cinderella. Throughout the age range, Charlie pretended most extensively with his miniature replicas of animals, trains, pirates, and cowboys. Both Kathy and Charlie enjoyed warm and loving relationships with their mothers and eagerly shared their imaginary worlds. In addition, Kathy was fortunate to have the company of other children, particularly a tolerant older sister. In Kathy, we see a common pattern of pretend play emerging from an adult-child activity in older infancy and toddlerhood, to a predominantly child-child activity in the preschool years. At forty-eight months, Pricilla prompted Kathy to pretend with other children, but filled in as play partner when other children were not available. In Charlie's family, child partners were not available, but this did not impoverish his play. He continued to flourish and develop as a pretender, creating elaborate performances alone and with his parents.

Finally, the portraits of Kathy and Charlie provide a glimpse of how pretend play is embedded in the lives of young children. Both Sandy and Pricilla spontaneously commented on the importance of staying at home with their young children. Indeed, both had put aside their own careers to do so. These were mothers who spent a great deal of time alone with their children, often inside their homes. They seemed to relish pretending, enjoying it for its own sake. Pretend play also provided a standby to cheer up bored and cranky children, enliven daily routines, defuse conflict, and communicate feelings.

10

Conclusions

The objective of this study was to address some fundamental descriptive and theoretical issues related to everyday pretending in sociocultural context. By following nine young children as they went about their ordinary activities in and around the home, we discovered that pretending was an important part of their daily lives. They spent a significant amount of time engaged in this activity, which served simultaneously as a mode of relating to significant others and as a vehicle for expressing individuality. Our most important findings concern the social nature of early pretending. From its inception pretend play was social—in the physical settings and cultural practices in which it was embedded, in its conduct with a partner, and in a variety of functions that it served. In this chapter we review and interpret the major findings of the study, delineate their theoretical implications, and point to promising areas for future research.

Amount of Pretending

In keeping with Piaget's (1962) original description and with subsequent reports in the literature (see Rubin, Fein, and Vandenberg 1983), pretending was infrequent and fleeting at twelve months of age. Observations of the same children at twenty-four, thirty-six, and forty-eight months showed an increase with age, thus providing long-range longitudinal evidence corroborating Piaget's claim that pretend play increases in frequency during the preschool years. By forty-eight months of age the children were prolific pretenders, spending an average of 12.4 minutes per hour pretending. Extrapolating across the day (excluding evenings), this amounts to nearly two hours per day of pretend activity. As they got older, the children not only engaged in more pretending but produced longer episodes, suggesting an increase both in the inclination to pretend and in the complexity and elaboration of episodes.

Ecological Context and Cultural Practices

Everyday pretending was embedded in a distinctive physical and social ecology and in a set of related cultural practices. These offspring of affluent, professional parents lived in spacious homes or apartments, which often included a playroom and a separate bedroom for each child. Once they were beyond the toddler stage, the children were free to range throughout the living space. Across the age span, however, most pretend play occurred in communal rooms, particularly livingrooms, playrooms, and kitchens.

Pretending flourished in the thick of family life—while an older sibling watched TV nearby or did homework with a friend, while mother folded laundry or set the table. This is not to say that private space was unused: at times quiet solo pretending or intimate play with a close friend or sibling unfolded in seclusion. But for the most part, pretending occurred in public spaces, where play partners could be readily recruited and mundane activities appropriated.

Pretending was framed not only by the physical space but by particular social configurations and practices. As the breadwinners in the families, fathers were absent during weekday mornings and afternoons, whereas mothers, as the primary caregivers, were invariably present. Eight of the nine children in the study had one or two siblings, but, at the early ages, access to siblings and other children was limited compared with access to mothers: older siblings were at school or engaged in activities in another part of the house, and non-kin peers were not available to the target chilren on a regular basis. As they grew older, their mothers were more likely to arrange for them to have peer experience and less likely to remain in the same room as the child played with a friend or sibling. Our finding that mothers were the primary play partners through thirty-six months thus reflects, in part, social ecological factors that maximize the availability of mothers as potential interactants. A preliminary finding suggests that children also may *prefer* to pretend with mothers at the younger ages, and this is consistent with previous reports of low levels of pretend play with peers during the third year of life (Sachs, Goldman, and Chaille, 1985). Future studies need to address the relative contribution of availability vs. preference in accounting for the mother's status as primary play partner in this cultural group.

Object Use as Cultural Practice

Everyday pretending was an activity that was mediated by objects, primarily realistic objects. This finding is interpretable from two different vantage points. First, it can be understood as a cultural practice initiated and sustained by parents that reflects the positive value placed upon play in this community. Every child in the study possessed a large quantity of child-scaled replica toys designed to be used in pretend play. By contrast, such objects are scarce (e.g., Trackton: Heath 1983) or nonexistent (e.g., Yucatec Maya: Gaskins 1990) in other cultural groups. Although some parts of the living space were defined as child space (playrooms, children's bedrooms) and were equipped with shelves and boxes for storage, toys spread inevitably beyond those boundaries. Parents sometimes complained of the clutter, but this did not deter them from providing a continually renewed supply of toys. This parental practice thus had the effect of creating for the child a physical environment heavily populated by the kinds of objects that have been found in previous studies to support children's early efforts at pretending, and to indirectly communicate the importance of play to children. Moreover, mothers did more than simply make objects available; they incorporated them into pretend interactions with the child. Even their early pretend overtures to twelve month olds—animating stuffed animals or speaking in high-pitched voices for dolls—were mediated by objects.

The use of objects in pretend play also bears examination from the child's standpoint. The importance of objects as a resource for pretending depended not just on adult participation in cultural practices but on children's active collusion in those practices. Parents made objects available; children appropriated them. Each child pretended with a diversity of objects while also favoring a particular object or objects—Kathy's North Star pony, Justin's trucks, Molly and Rachael's Tropical Skipper doll—that seemed to have special meaning, inspiring frequent, lengthy, or highly imaginative pretending. Charlie's zoo train retained its special status for several years, and Nancy's mother fondly recalled playing in the "ice-cream store" with Nancy's older brother. Although the children were able to substitute one object for another (e.g., a cup for a hat) by twenty-four months of age, they continued to pretend with replica objects through forty-eight months of age—the age at which peers rivalled mothers as play partners. Thus, in the later preschool years replica objects may provide an important bridge into peer relations, serving as reference points around which the shared meanings of peer culture are created and sustained.

Although replica objects figured centrally in the pretend play of the children we studied, we do not intend to imply that specialized objects or play spaces are necessary for the development of pretend play. Schwartzman (1986) observes that although in most societies children do not have their own private space (at least not interior space) or specialized play objects, they are able to construct active play lives for themselves. Children transform various types of environments into play areas of their own design, using what may seem to be useless and even dangerous space and materials (such as trash heaps and abandoned buildings) in very creative ways (Dargan and Zeitlin 1990). In a similar way, children are able to use whatever materials are available to create a variety of playthings.

For those children who do possess elaborate play props, the possibility arises that this cultural practice serves functions other than the support of pretend transformations or the mediation of peer relations. Our culture is a materialistic one that places a great deal of emphasis on ownership. Status and identity are closely linked to one's ability to possess scarce, expensive, and coveted objects. Within this framework, toys sometimes take on greater importance than mere playthings; they can be objects of status. The cultural practice of supplying children with toys also may communicate love, aspirations, and anxieties; and be related to many larger cultural patterns in the family, school, and marketplace (Sutton-Smith 1986). For example, the gift of certain "educational toys" may be possible because of technological advances in computer software, reflect beliefs about the relationship between toys and achievement, communicate the importance of achievement within the family, and be presented at birthdays as a token of love.

The Social Development of Pretending

Everyday pretending emerged as social not only in the settings and cultural practices in which it was embedded, but in the interpersonal character of the activity itself. We found that everyday pretending occurred predominantly in interaction with others during the entire period of emergence and early development, with mothers serving as the primary play partners. There were, however, systematic changes during this period in the behavior of both the children and their play partners.

At twelve months all of the mothers directed pretend play to their children, although pretending had emerged only barely in some children and not at all in others. Virtually any child pretending that occurred at this age was initiated by the mothers, and most of the verbal responses made by the children were reproductions of the mothers' verbalizations.

By twenty-four months pretending was fully and jointly established. Children and mothers pretended fluently with one another, and children as well as mothers sought out and responded to each other as play partners. Indeed, this seemed to be a pivotal time for mother-child pretending, with mothers and children showing maximal mutual involvement in joint pretending. There was remarkable consistency across individuals in that social pretending occurred exclusively with mothers for five children and primarily with mothers for another three children. At this age mothers responded contingently to their children's pretend contributions and provided elaborations and prompts at high rates. Pretend episodes with mothers were twice as long as solo episodes, and 30 percent of children's utterances within pretend play were reproductions of their mothers' pretend verbalizations.

At thirty-six and forty-eight months the overall amount of mother-child pretending did not decline although there was a decline in the proportion of social pretending involving mothers as play partners. Children and mothers continued to seek out each other as play partners and to respond at high rates to the other's initiations, and mothers continued to elaborate on and prompt children's pretend contributions. At these ages, however, the children reproduced little of their mothers' pretend talk. Moreover, at forty-eight months of age, pretend play seemed to be shifting toward the peer domain. The children pretended roughly equally with mothers and peers (siblings, friends), and now pretend episodes with peers were twice as long as solo episodes, which, in turn, were twice as long as episodes with mothers.

The Socialization of Pretending

Socialization has been described as the process by which caregivers structure the social environment and display patterned meanings for the novice (Wentworth 1980; Miller and Sperry 1988). Acquisition is the process by which the novice interprets, responds to, and ultimately is or is not affected by the social patterns to which he or she is exposed. Our study has the most to say about socialization in that it provides a culturally situated description of the interpersonal context in which early pretending occurs. This description of the interpersonal conduct of everyday pretending is significant first of all as an existence proof, showing that mothers in one cultural community routinely engage in pretend play with their young children and that their participation changes systematically over the preschool years. The strength of this existence proof, however, hinges on the degree to which our observations are ecologically valid for the particular families involved and whether these families are representative of this particular cultural group.

To address the first of these issues we must consider whether the observational procedure itself distorted our estimation of the nature and extent of caregiver involvement in children's pretending. Because the data were originally collected for a different purpose, awareness that pretend play was the focus of inquiry can be ruled out as a source of distortion. However, mothers were obviously aware of being observed and this may have affected the extent or nature of their participation in pretending. There are two factors that minimize these effects: the care that was taken to establish rapport with the families and the number and length of the observation sessions. Each family was observed for a total of seven sessions, each lasting three to four hours. It seems unlikely that mothers could sustain markedly altered patterns of interactions, especially with very young children, over such extended periods. The success of our efforts to capture "natural" behavior is suggested by the fact that subsequent to the first few minutes of observation, mothers and children rarely addressed the observer or oriented towards the camera. In addition, mothers and children engaged in numerous behaviors typically considered private including extended and intense conflicts (Haight and Garvey 1991).

Second, how representative is our sample of affluent, educated American families? Families were not recruited with the intention of studying pretend play, so it is unlikely that their pretend play per se is different from other members of their community. Indeed, while the mothers in our study showed a level of involvement in their children's pretending that would not be expected given the existing literature, the children were not precocious pretenders. Their attainment of the major developmental milestones of pretending was normative, e.g., pretend play was barely established at twelve months, and explicit role transformations did not appear until approximately thirty-six months. In addition, in agreement with Piaget (1962), pretend play with other children was a relatively late development.

We also believe that observations of mothers in everyday domestic settings are more likely to yield an accurate picture of their involvement in pretending than are the more typical laboratory-based observations. Indeed, our findings are consistent with the growing body of evidence that mothers in some cultural groups systematically introduce the pretend mode during the early years of their children's lives (Dunn and Wooding 1977; Kavanaugh, Whittington, and Cerbone 1983; Miller and Garvey 1984; Sachs 1980). Haight and Parke (in progress) found that during freeplay sessions in their homes, nearly all fifty middle-class parents of twenty-four month olds pretended with their young children, although there was tremendous variation in the extent and quality of their participation. During in-depth interviews these same parents reported engaging in pretend play with their children from several times a week to many times a day.

While the finding that mothers from any cultural group participate routinely in their children's pretending is significant, future research must explore in more depth and detail variation across social and cultural groups. Current theories of pretend play are theories of middle-class, European American play. Although the anthropological literature contains numerous references to pretend play (Schwartzman 1978), only recently have cross-cultural studies been undertaken with pretend play as the focus of investigation (e.g., Gaskins 1990; Goncu and Mosier 1991; Farver 1991; Zukow 1989). These newer studies provide the ecological and ethnographic detail necessary for culturally sophisticated comparisons of pretending and suggest that pretending differs across cultures at multiple levels of analysis.

The Acquisition of Pretending

Although our study has the most to say about socialization, our findings also have implications for acquisition. Many studies implicitly assume that caregivers do not participate in early pretending or that such participation is irrelevant to the development of pretending. These assumptions are grounded in a theoretical orientation in which the emergence of pretend play is seen as a spontaneous by-product of symbolic thought (Piaget 1962). The fact that the mothers in our study were involved extensively in their children's early pretend play, however, compels us to *consider* a heretofore ignored alternative theoretical formulation for the acquisition of pretending; namely, that other people have some role in its emergence and early elaboration.

Clearly, our finding that caregivers participate in children's early pretending does not indicate that such participation is necessary for, or even facilitative of, pretending. Caregiver-child pretend play may simply be a mutually enjoyable mode of interaction that contributes little to children's emerging abilities to pretend. Indeed, Isaacs (1937) recognized that mothers do participate in their young children's pretend play but discounted that involvement on the assumption that mothers were either passive or dominating play partners. Our data clearly contradict Issacs' claims. Pretend interactions were constructed according to norms of mutuality: both mothers and children initiated and responded to pretending, and mothers elaborated upon and prompted children's pretending. Furthermore, our data do suggest that participation of a caregiver has an immediate effect upon the structure of children's episodes of pretend play and upon their pretend transformations. Episodes of pretend play involving mothers were more sustained than solo pretend play (see Dunn and Wooding 1977; Slade 1987) through thirty-six months. In addition, at the younger ages, children incorporated a substantial proportion of their mothers' pretend talk into their own subsequent play.

Although these findings suggest that mothers' participation has an immediate impact on children's pretending, particularly during children's entry into pretend play, future research must examine more extended outcomes. In particular, future work needs to explore possible links between individual variation in mothers' participation and individual variation in their children's pretending. Our findings point to considerable consistency within this socioeconomically homogeneous sample of mothers in the main outlines of our findings, but there were some striking individual differences in the amount of mother participation, and these may account, in part, for differences in the children. There were also some obvious qualitative differences in mothers' enjoyment of pretending and in their imaginativeness, and these deserve further investigation in relation to variation in children's pretending.

Problems for Theory

These findings concerning the socialization and acquisition of pretend play pose significant problems for theories of pretending. Although socialization and acquisition are analytically separable processes, we believe that they are related and mutually influential. The challenge for theory is to specify the exact nature of that relationship.

For example, how can we account in a principled way for the play partner's contribution to the emergence and early development of pretend play? Neither Piaget nor Freud provides a solution to this problem. Vygotskian theory is more promising in that it offers a general account of the interpersonal origins of higher psychological functions, but in his writing on pretend play Vygotsky (1978) did not articulate how this general principle of development is instantiated in pretending. For example, to what extent does the socialization into pretend play mediate subsequent symbolic development? Children's emerging symbolic capacities may be recruited into a variety of conventionalized expressive systems including pretend play. Indeed, pretend play was quite popular among our European American mothers. Other communities may emphasize teasing, ritual, etc. The extent to which particular cultural communities emphasize particular expressive systems may shape the development of children's emerging symbolic, expressive capacities.

A second problem for theories of pretend play is related to the first and centers on variation in pretend play. Despite the homogeneity of our sample, we found individual variation on a number of important quantitative and qualitative parameters. Moreover, when we compare our findings to other cultural cases (e.g., Gaskins 1989, 1990; Heath 1983; Schwartzman

1978; Zukow 1989; Goncu and Mosier 1991), dramatic cross-cultural variation is evident in the amount and complexity of pretending, in the type and availability of play props, and in the participation of parents and older children in pretend play with novices. Current theories cannot account for either individual or cross-cultural variation in pretending nor can they explain how environmental factors (e.g., types of play partners, role of play props) contribute to variation (Gaskins and Goncu 1988).

Parental Beliefs about Pretending

One possible source of individual and cross-cultural variation in parental involvement in pretend play is the belief systems that frame and inform parental actions. During extensive interviews with fifty middle-class European American parents, Haight (1991) found that both mothers and fathers rate pretend play as important to their children's development; they believe that their participation facilitates children's pretending; and they can articulate distinct reasons for how pretending facilitates development. For example, in striking agreement with psychoanalytic theories, many of the parents considered pretending to be an important expressive vehicle for young children. Many also expressed a great deal of personal enjoyment in pretending. Jane, a clerical worker and mother of thirty-month-old Mary explains, "It's—I think it's helping her build a great personality. She can express herself." (She goes on to describe that if Mary is upset over something, she hears about it during their pretend play.) "I guess I pretended a lot when I was little. Frank (husband) sometimes says I had a child just to have a playmate . . . I LOVE to pretend play!"

In agreement with Vygotsky, many parents also mentioned the value of pretend play in gratifying young children. For example, Jim, a medical student and father of Matthew explained that when he is unable to play with Matthew, Matthew will play with an imaginary companion. "Last night when I was fixing dinner, Matthew wanted me to play with him.

When I explained that I couldn't he began ice skating around the kitchen with Little Rono."

Also in agreement with Vygotsky, many parents expressed the belief that pretending helps children to explore everyday situations and social roles. Many also felt that this learning is facilitated by the participation of a parent. For example, Tom, an elementary school teacher and father of thirty-month-old Steven, explained:

> ... Pretending is the work of children. They—I think he gains a good sense of the world by putting himself into different characters. . . . That's how he develops a sense of. . . his role in the world and the role of others. It allows him to put himself into other's shoes. . . . He pretends a lot with me as, as a boy. And with his father he pretends a lot of male roles, father-type roles. He picks up on those things from me. And so going through the phases, the process of thinking and pretending to mow the lawn, and fixing the sink and putting together the stereo or painting the house—those sorts of things—to help him identify a male image for himself. Very important.

In agreement with Vygotsky and Piaget, many parents also stressed the value of pretending for developing the imagination. For example, Fred, a repairman and father of two-year-old Andy, stressed that pretending develops the imagination. "Imagination is everything. Without imagination you can't go far. Building his imagination is real important and I can help him with that as . . . [his loving] parent."

Other parents, like Piaget, valued pretending primarily for the glimpse it provides them into their children's minds. For example, Kevin, a contractor and father of twenty-four-month-old Ann, explains, "It's a chance for parents or adults to let them come up with something. . . [Pretending is a] little window to what their minds are doing. . . "

Although their beliefs about the developmental significance of pretend play were similar in broad outline, this homogeneous sample of middle-class American parents also showed individual variation, and this variation was related to the extent of their reported involvement in pretending. There is some additional evidence of individual and cultural variation in parents' beliefs about pretending and their related practices. In their study of British mothers and children, Tizard and Hughes (1984) report that most middle-class mothers expressed the belief that pretend play was educational and were observed to actually participate in their children's pretending. In contrast, fewer working-class mothers viewed pretend play as educational and tended to participate with their children in other types of play. Newson and Newson (1979) also report that a minority of British working-class mothers disliked and disapproved of their four year olds' pretend play, and Dunn (1986) reports that it was less common for children in her lowest social-class groups to pretend with their mothers.

Comparative studies of pretend play also suggest variation in parents' perceptions of the importance of pretending and their related practices. Farver (1991) observed American and Mexican mothers and their young children. She reports that American mothers value play activity for its potential contribution to their children's intellectual and socioemotional growth, and often involved their children in elaborate pretend play. In contrast, Mexican mothers who stress the acquisition of social skills and the development of productive work habits promote these behaviors by including their young children in the daily routine of adult work activity. Goncu and Mosier (1991) observed that middle-class Americans and Turkish parents think of themselves as play partners for their children, while Mayan Indians and tribal Indians think of play as a children's activity. Evidence of individual and cultural variation in parental beliefs about play suggests that theories of pretend play need to take into account the conventionalized but variable parental beliefs and related practices that frame the everyday context of pretending.

Methodological Implications

In addition to the theoretical problems raised by our findings, there are some important methodological implications of the study. Because our observation sessions were unusually long we were able to analyze how pretend play was distributed across the several hours of observation. We found that the bulk of pretending occurred after the first hour of observation at thirty-six and forty-eight months of age. This suggests that more attention should be paid to the length of time necessary to obtain valid samples of pretending at different ages. Shorter observation sessions may be quite adequate for sampling the brief pretend episodes of two year olds, but may underestimate the amount and complexity of pretending in older pre-schoolers. At older ages, children may need more time to ha-bituate to the presence of the observer, or they may need more uninterrupted time to elaborate pretend themes satisfactorily.

A second and related issue concerns the need for more research that captures pretend episodes in their entirety. The children in this study showed an increase not only in the amount of pretending but in the length of pretend episodes. Without further naturalistic studies of episodes as they unfold, it will be difficult to identify those processes internal to epi-sodes that account for the lengthening of episodes. Sequential analyses within pretend episodes is also necessary for further understanding of the interactive properties of joint episodes. For example, the present study established that, at younger ages, children imitated their mothers during pretend play, but imitations are a crude measure of the extent to which children incorporate caregivers' ideas for pretend play into their own subsequent play. A more detailed look at the thematic contin-gencies between mothers' pretend talk and children's re-sponses is required.

Other Promising Areas for Future Research

The findings of our study are relevant to a number of ongoing problems which have been addressed through laboratory re-search, e.g., the length of episodes of solo versus social pretend-ing. Our focus on pretending in its everyday contexts, however, reveals a number of unique problems relevant to the social functions of pretending. In chapter 7, we noted the power of pretending as an expressive vehicle and tool in influ-encing others' behavior. We suggested that in everyday life pretending can function to communicate feelings, to muster an argument, to enliven daily routiness, to teach and just to have fun. Future research needs to examine systematically the contexts from which everyday pretending arises, as well as the everyday contexts which are incorporated into pretend play. In addition, closer attention is needed to the themes of caregiver-child pretend play.

Conclusion

We conclude that our findings—based as they are on unusually extensive, ecologically valid observations—provide the strongest support to date that mothers in this cultural group pretend extensively with their children during the early years. These findings not only point to directions for future research but also challenge theories of pretend play to account for the role of the sociocultural context in the emergence and early development of pretend play.

Appendix A

Subcategories of Pretending

A sound measure of pretend play is required if we are to find answers to basic issues including the social nature of early pretending. Children's pretending typically enacted stories. They also pretended with objects they had constructed, and told narratives of past pretending. Even when the pretend episode was abbreviated, children's communications of their intentions to pretend were usually clear. Children under the age of thirty-six months also elaborated stories in their pretending, especially when collaborating with a more experienced pretender. More frequent at the younger than the older ages, however, were episodes of pretending that were fleeting and less elaborated. These episodes included single actions of pretending or sequences of actions that did not tell a story, or the incorporation of pretending into ritual play.

Abbreviated Pretending.

Occasionally, particularly during early peer play, children would propose pretend play, but no enactment followed. For example, thirty-six-month-old Kathy proposed to her friend,

"I'll be the Mommy." The friend agreed, but no enactment followed.

Single Actions and Sequences.

Consistent with previous descriptions (e.g., see Rubin, Fein, and Vandenberg 1983), the pretending we observed in the second year of life was extremely fleeting and consisted primarily of single actions. For example, twelve-month-old Kathy said, "Hi" while gazing into the face of her stuffed bear. Late in the second year, and early in the third year, children produced series of pretend actions identical to those described by Piaget (1962) and Nicolich (1977). They describe single-scheme combinations, emerging at around one and a half years, during which a single pretend action is applied to several different receivers of the action, e.g., a child drinks from a cup, then feeds the doll from a cup. Nicolich also describes multischeme combinations, emerging at approximately one and a half to two years, in which several schemes are related to one another in sequence without regard for their logical order. For example, the child "feeds" the doll, then "heats" the bottle on a toy stove. In our study, twenty-month-old Elizabeth "drank" from a cup, and then "poured" from the pitcher while successively emptying a set of toy dishes from their box.

Ritual Pretending.

Another pattern that we observed early in the third year of life was the extension of pretending through rituals. For example, twenty-four-month-old Nancy approached her mother and directed, "Mommy cry." Her mother then enacted crying. Next, her mother suggested, "Nancy cry" and Nancy imitated her mother's cry. Nancy then requested, "Mommy be happy," at which point her mother pretended to laugh. Then her mother requested, "Nancy be happy," and Nancy imitated her mother's pretend laugh. This round was repeated several times. Another example from this same pair occurred as twenty-four-month-old Nancy sat on her mother's lap listening to *Snow White and the Seven Dwarfs* (including Sneezy). She looked at her mother and said, "Ah choo!!" while vigorously nodding her head. Her mother responded by imitating the sneeze and nod. Nancy initiated the "Ah choo!" sequence with her mother several times over the next few minutes.

Prototypic Pretending with a Story.

When we think of pretending, most of us would recall an episode similar to Kathy's adventures with North Star and Superhair which seems to "tell a story." They consist of sequences of two or more different but thematically related actions of pretend play. They form a routine, are logically related, or are consistent with previously established roles or themes. Consistent with previous descriptions (e.g., see Rubin, Fein, and Vandenberg 1983; Nicolich 1977), after approximately twenty-four months of age the children in our study frequently produced such prototypic episodes. For example, thirty-six-month-old Molly offered her five-year-old sister, Rachael (the "baby"), a bottle, announced that the baby was sick, fed her some medicine and, finally, left for work. A second example is thirty-six-month-old Charlie's train play: he pushed a toy train to accompanying sound effects, occasionally stopping to let on pretend passengers (Fisher-Price figures) while ordering, "All aboard." Another example is the soccer game initiated by thirty-six-month-old Nancy who announced to her mother, "I'm a soccer player. . . . You're a soccer player too." The "soccer players" preceded to hit a black balloon back and forth, note their "touchdowns," etc.

Pretending with Constructions.

As children became involved in constructing things with materials (i.e., gluing, molding, stacking, or otherwise assembling), these creations were incorporated into pretend play. Note that the actual process of construction was not considered pretend play unless accompanied by clear dramatizations. For example, thirty-six-month-old John constructed a castle out of Legos, and this was not considered pretending. We did consider it pretending, however, when he subsequently made his

Fisher-Price figure climb up the tower, knock on the door and ask, "Anybody home?"

Narratives of Pretending.

Sometimes children produced narratives of pretend play, recounting earlier episodes of pretend play in which they participated, or describing the adventures of some other real or fictional person. While these episodes were more typical of children from the age of thirty-six months, they were observed in younger children as well. For example, twenty-four-month-old Molly, climbing on top of some playground equipment, paused to relate events of play occurring several days earlier including: "Catherine fall down. Sharks down there." Another example occurred at thirty-six months, when Molly's five-year-old sister, Rachael, mentioned a visit with some friends, and Molly added, ". . . And Chris was my baby and I was Chris's mommy." A third example occurred when forty-eight month-old Kathy stood holding her doll, recounting how, yesterday, the doll fell into a hole and was eventually rescued.

Appendix B

Ambiguous Actions Excluded from Analyses
of Pretending

The following types of actions were excluded because their pretend status was ambiguous:

1. Play suggested by the attributes of replica objects. Children sometimes produced actions that were suggested by the object's unique and salient physical characteristic (see Rocissano 1982). For example, twenty-four-month-old Molly held a doll by the arm, twelve-month-old Kathy put a toy biscuit into a toy bowl, and twelve-month-old John pushed a toy car. In the absence of other relevant verbal or nonverbal enactments such actions were excluded.

2. Labeling replica objects. Children also produced conventional labels for toy replicas without accompanying pretend enactment. For example, we excluded twenty-four-month-old Molly's reference to a baby doll as the "baby."

3. Ritual hide and seek games. Younger children enjoyed a variety of games, often highly ritualized, involving hidden objects or persons. While such games frequently included feigned surprise or concern, all hiding games were excluded. For example, twelve-month-old Nancy's mother placed a toy

into a container and then asked, dramatically, "Where is it?" Twenty-four-month-old Nancy hid beneath the table in view of her mother. Her mother called out in an exaggerated, distressed voice: "Where's Nancy? Where's Nancy?"

4. Sports play. Sports play was more typical of the children as preschoolers. We observed children using child-sized sports equipment as they would the corresponding full-scale objects. Such actions sometimes were preceded or accompanied by verbal descriptions, e.g., "I'm playing baseball." These actions were only included as pretend play if they co-occurred with clear gestures of enactment, e.g., gesturing as if catching an imaginary ball, or transformational statements, e.g., "I'm a Chicago Bears!" For example, we excluded thirty-six-month-old Michael's play as he threw a miniature basketball towards a miniature hoop while announcing, "I'm playing basketball." We also excluded the play of thirty-six-month-old John as he pedaled around the patio on a "bat mobile" bike.

5. Stage-setting. "Stage-setting" activities were more typical of the children as preschoolers. These activities included arranging toy replicas such as doll-house furniture. Such actions were excluded when they were unaccompanied by transformational actions or talk. For example, we excluded the actions of twenty-four-month-old Elizabeth as she placed toy furniture in a doll-house while her mother labeled them. Arranging the doll house furniture while discussing where the baby would sleep would have been included as pretend play.

6. Literacy activites. Children also engaged in a wide range of symbolic, literacy-related activites such as book reading, story telling, drawing, and singing. For example, twenty-four-month-old Molly and her mother sang, "The eensey-weensey spider" with accompanying gestures. These activites sometimes even contained imaginary elements. For example, thirty-six-month-old Kathy referred to the girl in her drawing: "She likes pink hair." All literacy-related activities were excluded, however, unless they were clearly part of the pretend play, as when forty-eight-month-old Nancy and her friend, while playing school, pretended to write stories.

7. Decontextualized demonstrations. Occasionally children produced decontextualized actions in contexts that clearly were not play. For example, we excluded forty-eight-month-old Charlie's demonstration of how firefighters, observed earlier on "Sesame Street", spray water.

References

Bateson, G. (1956). The message "This is play." In *Group Processes*, edited by B. Schaffner, New York: Josiah Macy.

Bauman, R. and J. Sherzer (1989). Preface. In *Explorations in the ethnography of speaking*. Second edition, Cambridge: Cambridge University Press.

Beizer, L. (1991) "Preverbal precursors of pretend play: Developmental and cultural dimensions." Paper presented at the biannual meeting of the Society for Research in Child Development, Seattle.

Bloom, L., L. Rocissano, and L. Hood (1976). Adult-child discourse: Developmental interaction between information processing and linguistic knowledge. *Cognitive Psychology* 8: 521–52.

Clarke-Stewart, K. A. (1978). And daddy makes three: The father's impact on the mother and young child. *Child Development* 49: 466–478.

Crawley, S. B. and K. B. Sherrod (1984). Parent-infant play during the first year of life. *Infant Behavior and Development* 7(1): 65–75.

Dale, N. (1983). "Early pretend play in the family." Unpublished doctoral dissertation, University of Cambridge, Cambridge, England.

Dargan, A. and S. Zeitlin (1990). *City play.* New Brunswick: Rutgers University Press.

Dunn, J. (1986). Pretend play in the family. In *Play interactions: The contribution of play materials and parental involvement to children's development,* edited by A. W. Gottfried and C. C. Brown. Lexington, Mass.: Lexington Books.

_____. (1988). *The beginnings of social understanding.* Cambridge, Mass.: Harvard University Press.

Dunn, J. and N. Dale, (1984). I a daddy: 2-year-olds' collaboration in joint pretend with sibling and with mother. In *Symbolic play: The development of social understanding,* edited by I. Bretherton. New York: Academic Press.

Dunn, J. and C. Wooding (1977). Play in the home and its implications for learning. In *Biology of play,* edited by B. Tizard and D. Harvey. London: Heinemann.

El'Konin, D. (1966). Symbolics and its functions in the play of children. *Soviet Education* 8: 35–41.

Emmerich, W. (1977). Evaluating alternative models of development: An illustrative study of preschool personal-social behavior. *Child Development* 48: 1401–10.

Farver, J. (1991). "Cultural differences in scaffolding pretend play: A comparison of American and Mexican American mother-child and sibling-child pairs." Paper presented at the biannual meeting of the Society for Research in Child Development, Seattle.

Fein, G. (1981). Pretend play: An integrative review. *Child Development,* 52: 1095–1118.

Fein, G. and N. Apfel (1979). Some preliminary observations on knowing and pretending. In *Symbolic functioning in childhood.* edited by N. Smith and M. Franklin. Hillsdale, N.J.: Erlbaum.

Fenson, L., J. Kagan, R. B. Kearsley, and P. R. Zelazo (1976). The developmental progression of manipulative play in the first two years. *Child Development* 47: 232–235.

Fiese, B. (1987). "Mother-infant interaction and symbolic play in the second year of life: A contextual analysis." Paper presented at the biannual meeting of the Society for Research in Child Development.

Garvey, C. (1982). Communication and the development of social role play. In *New directions in child development: The development of planful behavior in children,* edited by D. Forbes and M. Greenberg. San Fransisco: Jossey-Bass.

_____. (1990). *Play.* Cambridge, Mass.: Harvard University Press.

Garvey, C. and T. Kramer (1989). The language of social pretend play. *Developmental Review* 9: 364–82.

Garvey, C. and C. Shantz (1992). Varieties of conflict and development: A Sociolinguistic perspective. In C. U. Shantz and W. W. Hartup (Eds.) *Conflict in child and adolescent development.* Cambridge: Cambridge University Press.

Gaskins, S. (1989 Feb.). "Symbolic play in a Mayan village." Paper presented at the annual meeting of the Association for the Study of Play, Philadelphia.

_____. (1990) "Exploration and development in Mayan infants" Ph.D. dissertation, University of Chicago.

Gaskins, S. and A. Goncu (1988). "Children's play as representation and imagination: The case of Piaget and Vygotsky." *The Quarterly Newsletter at the Laboratory of Human Cognition,* 10: 104–7.

Goncu, A. and C. Mosier (1991). "Cultural variations in the play of toddlers." Paper presented at the biannual meeting of the Society for Research in Child Development, Seattle.

Goncu, A., B. Rogoff and J. Mistry (July 1989) Cultural variations in the play of toddlers. International Society for the Study of Behavioral Development. Finland.

Goodnow J. J. (1990). The socialization of cognition: What's involved? In *Cultural Psychology,* edited by J. W. Stigler, R. A. Schweder and G. Herdt. Cambridge: Cambridge University Press.

Haight, W. (1989). "The ecology and development of pretend play from one to four years of age." Ph.D. dissertation, University of Chicago.

_____. (April 1991). "Belief systems that frame and inform parental participation in their children's pretend play." Paper presented at the biannual meeting of the Society for Research in Child Development, Seattle, Washington.

Haight, W. and C. Garvey (April 1991). "Caregiver-child interaction and the emergence of young children's conflict repertoires." Paper presented at the biannual meeting of the Society for Research in Child Development, Seattle, Washington.

Haight, W. and R. Parke (In progress). Play with mothers, fathers and friends during the third year of life.

Heath, S. B. (1983). *Ways with words: Langauge, life and work in communities and classrooms.* Cambridge, England: Cambridge University Press.

Hetherington, M., M. Cox and R. Cox (1979). Play and social interaction in children following divorce. *Journal of Social Issues* 35: 26–49.

Howes, C. (1985). Sharing fantasy: Social pretend play in toddlers. *Child Development* 56: 1253–58.

Isaacs, S. (1937). Social development in young children: A study of the beginnings. New York: Harcourt, Brace and Company.

Kavanaugh, R. D., S. Whittington and M. J. Cerbone (1983). Mothers' use of fantasy in speech to young children. *Journal of Child Language* 10: 45–55.

Lamb, M. (1977). Father-infant and mother-infant interaction in the first year of life. *Child Development* 48: 167–181.

MacDonald, K. and R. Parke (1986). Parent-child physical play: The effects of sex and age of children and parents. *Sex Roles* 15: 367–78.

McLoyd, V. (1983). The effects of the structure of play objects on the pretend play of low-income preschool children. *Child Development* 54: 626–35.

Manwell E. M. and A. G. Mengert (1934). A study of the development of two- and three-year-old children with respect to play activities. *University of Iowa Studies on Child Welfare* 9: 67–111.

Miller, P. and C. Garvey (1984). Mother-baby role play: Its origins in social support. In *Symbolic play: The development of social understanding*, edited by I. Bretherton. Orlando, Fl: Academic Press.

Miller, P. and L. Sperry (1988) Early talk about the past. The origins of conversational stories of personal experience. *Journal of Child Language* 15: 293–315.

Montessori, M.(1973). *The Montessori method.* Cambridge, Mass.: Bentley, Inc.

New, R. (1982). "Traditional values and contemporary Italian infant care." Paper presented at the 81st annual meeting of the American Anthropological Association, Washington, D.C., December.

Newson, J. and E. Newson (1979). *Toys and Playthings.* New York: Pantheon Books.

Nicolich, L. (1977). Beyond sensorimotor intelligence: Assessment of symbolic maturity through analysis of pretend play. *Merrill-Palmer Quarterly*, 23, 89–99.

Ochs, E. and B. Schieffelin (1984). Language acquisition and socialization: Three developmental stories and their implications. In *Culture Theory: Essays on mind, self and emotion*, edited by R. A. Schweder and D. A. Levine. Cambridge Mass.: Cambridge University Press.

O'Connell, B. and I. Bretherton (1984). Toddler's play alone and with mother: The role of maternal guidance. In *Symbolic play: The development of social understanding*, edited by I. Bretherton. Orlando Fl: Academic Press.

Paley, V. (1984). *Boys and girls: Superheros in the doll corner.* Chicago: The University of Chicago Press.

Piaget, J. (1962). *Play, dreams and imitation in childhood.* New York: Norton.

Pulaski, M. (1973). Toys and imaginative play. In *The child's world of make-believe*, edited by J. L. Singer. New York: Academic Press.

Rheingold, H. L. and K. V. Cook (1975). The contents of boys' and girls' rooms as an index of parents behavior. *Child Development* 46: 459–63.

Rocissano, L. (1982). The emergence of social conventional behavior: Evidence from early object play. *Social Cognition* 1: 50–69.

Rogoff, B. (1990). *Apprenticeship in thinking: Cognitive development in social context.* New York: Oxford University Press.

Rogoff, B., C. Mosier, J. Mistry and A. Goncu (1991). Toddlers' guided participation with their caregivers in cultural activity in E. Forman, N. Minick and A. Stone (Eds.) *The Institutional and social context of mind.* New York: Oxford University Press.

Rosenblatt, D. (1977). Developmental trends in infant play. In B. Tizard & D. Harvey (Eds.), *The biology of play*, Philadelphia: Lippincott.

Rubin, K. H., G. G. Fein, and B. Vandenberg (1983). Play. In *Handbook of child psychology, Volume 3: Cognitive development*, edited by P. Mussen. New York: John Wiley and Sons.

Rubin, K. H., K. Watson, and T. Jambor (1978). Free play behaviors in preschool and kindergarten children. *Child Development* 49: 534–36.

Sachs, J. (1980). The role of adult-child play in language development. *New Directions for Child Development* 9: 33–48.

Sachs, J., J. Goldman, and C. Chaille (1984). Planning in pretend play: Using language to coordinate narrative development. In *The development of oral and written language in social contexts*, edited by A. D. Pellegrini and T. D. Yawkey. Norwood, N.J.: Ablex Publishing Corp.

_____. (1985). Narratives in preschoolers' sociodramatic play: The role of knowledge and communicative competence. In *Play, language and story: The development of children's literate behavior,* edited by L. Galda and A. Pellegrini. Norwood, N.J.: Ablex Publishing Corp.

Sanders, K. M. and L. V. Harper (1976). Free-play fantasy behavior in preschool children: Relations among gender, age, season, and location. *Child Development* 47: 1182–85.

Sapir E. (1934/1949). The emergence of the concept of personality in a study of cultures. D. G. Mandelbaum (Ed.). Selected writings of Edward Sapir in language, culture and personality. Berkeley: University of California Press.

Schwartzman, H. B. (1978). *Transformations: The anthropology of children's play.* New York: Plenum Press.

_____. (1980). Preface. In *Play and Culture,* edited by H. B. Schwartzman. West Point, N.Y. Leisure Press.

_____. (1986). A cross-cultural perspective on child-structured play activities and materials. In *Play interactions: The contribution of play materials and parental involvement to children's development,* edited by A. W. Gottfried and C. C. Brown. Lexington, Mass.: Lexington Books.

Singer, J. (Ed.). (1973). *The child's world of make-believe: Experimental studies of imaginative play.* New York: Academic Press.

Singer, D. and J. Singer (1990) *The house of make-believe: Children's play and the developing imagination.* Cambridge, Mass.: Harvard University Press.

Slade, A. (1987). A longitudinal study of maternal involvement and symbolic play during the toddler period. *Child Development* 58: 367–75.

Smolucha, F. (April 1989). "The relevance of Vygotsky's theory of creative imagination for contemporary research on play." Paper presented at the biannual meeting of the Society for Research in Child Development. Baltimore, Maryland.

Smolucha, F. (1991). The origins of object substitutions in social pretend play. Ph.D. dissertation, University of Chicago.

Sutton-Smith, B. (1986). *Toys as Culture.* New York: Gardner Press, Inc.

Tizard, B. and M. Hughes (1984). *Young children learning*. Cambridge, Mass.: Harvard University Press.

Valentine, C. W. (1937). A study of the beginnings and significance of play in infancy II. *British Journal of Educational Psychology* 8; 285.

Vandenberg, B. R. (1986). Beyond the ethology of play. In *Play interactions: The contribution of play materials and parental involvement to children's development,* edited by A. W. Gottfried and C. C. Brown. Lexington, Mass.: Lexington Books.

Vygotsky, L. S. (1962). *Thought and language*. Cambridge, Mass.: M.I.T. Press.

_____. (1978). *Mind in society: The development of higher mental processes*. Cambridge, Mass.: Harvard University Press.

Watson, M. and K. Fischer (1977). A developmental sequence of agent use in late infancy. *Child Development* 48: 828–836.

Wentworth, W. M. (1980). *Context and understanding: An inquiry into socialization theory*. New York: Elsevier.

Werner, H. and B. Kaplan (1963). *Symbol formation: An organismic-developmental approach to language and the expression of thought*. New York: John Wiley and Sons, Inc.

Whiting, B. B. and C. P. Edwards (1988). *Children of different worlds: The formation of social behavior*. Cambridge, Mass.: 1988.

Winnicott, D. W. (1971). *Playing and Reality*. London: Tavistock Publications Limited.

Wolfe, D. (1982). Understanding others: A longitudinal case study of the concept of independent agency. In *Action and thought,* edited by G. E. Forman. New York: Academic Press.

Wolfe, D., J. Rygh and J. Altshuler (1984). Agency and experience: Actions and states in play narratives. In *Symbolic play: The development of social understanding,* edited by I. Bretherton. Orlando, Fl: Academic Press.

Zukow, P. (1989). Siblings as effective socializing agents: Evidence from central Mexico. In *Sibling interaction across cultures: Theoretical and methodological issues,* edited by P. Zukow. New York: Springer-Verlag.

Author Index

Subject Index